PHYSICAL EDUCATION AND THE LAW

Dr. Herb Appenzeller
Athletic Director and
Professor of Education
Guilford College
Greensboro, North Carolina

THE MICHIE COMPANY
Law Publishers
CHARLOTTESVILLE, VIRGINIA

TO
E.C. BOLMEIER
TEACHER, COUNSELOR, FRIEND

ACKNOWLEDGMENTS

The writing of *Physical Education and the Law* has been made possible because many people cared and shared their ideas and efforts. Although it is impossible to mention each one individually, I am grateful, nevertheless for their help.

I wish especially to thank the following:

. . . . Dr. James Gifford for his outstanding assistance in the development, organization and style of the book and his willingness to give generously of his time in my behalf.

. . . . C. Thomas Ross, attorney with Craige, Brawley, Lipfert and Ross for his advice and suggestions regarding the legal aspects of the book.

. . . . Bynum Hunter, attorney and Amy Wilson, librarian, Smith, Moore, Smith, Schell, and Hunter.

. . . . Mary Lou Stone, librarian, Guilford County Law Library.

. . . . Wake Forest University Law Library.

. . . . Kenan Foundation for its support.

. . . . Sheila Kendall and Ann Johnson for typing the manuscripts.

. . . . To all the members of my family for their continued encouragement and support.

Herb Appenzeller

PREFACE

In 1975 I delivered a speech on the legal aspects of physical education at the National Convention of the American Alliance of Health, Physical Education and Recreation. After the talk, I visited the publisher's booth where my books *From the Gym to the Jury* (1970) and *Athletics and the Law* (1975) were on display.

That day in Milwaukee I heard "Hey mister, do either of these books have anything in them about kids drowning?" Before I could answer, the woman shook her head in disgust and continued, "I had a kid in my class go down the drain and now they are suing me." Just like that! matter of fact, with little or no remorse or compassion for the young boy who had drowned. If anything, there was a trace of bitterness in her voice because she was involved in an unpleasant lawsuit.

Minutes later I heard two physical education teachers whisper to each other how much the books terrified them. They admitted that they were so afraid of an injury and subsequent lawsuit that they attempted to eliminate any and all high risk activities.

Still later, a third opinion was reflected by several others who pointed to the books as helpful guides and necessary resources in their field. They stated that after reading the books they now felt comfortable and confident about their responsibility and work. They felt the legal parameters gave them a positive direction and a new awareness of the law that enabled them to be more effective teachers.

These experiences reinforced my opinion that there are three distinct categories in which most physical education teachers fall; namely, the apathetic, the anxious and the aware.

Apathetic teachers are just that, insensitive, indifferent and uninterested in knowing what is expected of a physical education professional. These teachers too frequently engage in "Russian Roulette" as they gamble with the safety and welfare of the students under their supervision. They blunder blindly along without the necessary concern for their students. An alarming allegation, admittedly, but one that exists too often, in too many places.

On the reverse side of the coin are the anxious and overcautious. These teachers mean well, in fact, they may be too conscientious. These teachers are so afraid of an accident that they try to eliminate every hazard and risk from their activities and games. Often all they eliminate are the activities themselves. These are the teachers who are responsible for the elimination of gymnastic exercises, use of the springboard and trampoline, and practically any high risk activity. While dedicated and careful, these teachers unknowingly are denying young people their rightful challenge of exciting programs.

Hopefully, the final group represents the majority of physical education teachers everywhere. These are the ones who realize that worthwhile activities have accompanying risks and that risks are normal. They recognize that while accidents do occur this does not necessarily mean lawsuits will follow, and if one should develop it doesn't necessarily mean they will be found guilty. So these teachers pursue their job eagerly, not avoiding challenges but looking for them. These are the people who meet their classes daily with confidence and as a result inspire their students through lively, challenging activities.

In writing *Physical Education and the Law,* I realize
that I could use unfavorable decisions and sky-rocketing
awards to frighten the apathetic. However, I expect the
effect, if any at all, would only be temporary. I also could
ease the minds of the anxious and overcautious by
giving them countless, reassuring instances of favorable
rulings by the court. But this too would probably be a
temporary solution again.

Instead, I am directing *Physical Education and the
Law* to all the loyal, dedicated teachers. I want to
present the decisions of the courts as frankly, openly and
realistically as possible so that I can reinforce their
attitude toward physical education and liability. After
all, these people continue to make physical education
what it should be or must become for our young people.
The students are ready! It is up to us to present them
with a challenging program that is safe and filled with
hope for the future.

CONTENTS

1. Negligence

The right of trial by jury is recognized in the
Magna Charta, our Declaration of Inde-
pendence and both our State and
Federal Constitutions. It is a
fundamental right in our
democratic judicial
system.[1]

Physical education teachers, administrators and school districts are sued for exorbitant damages as the number of lawsuits increases each year. Students are injured more often in physical education accidents than in any other school-related activity. Since the risk of injury is high in physical education, the courts regard many of the accidents as foreseeable. Therefore, activities conducted in the gymnasium or on the playground require the school to furnish supervision and formulate rules for safe conduct.

When you consider the high cost of awards for injuries you wonder who really pays the price for negligence. How many dedicated teachers will live a life filled with regret because a child entrusted to their care suffered serious injury? Could it be the parents who are forced to sit by helpless to do anything to restore their crippled child to normal health? Will it be the overburdened taxpayer who must meet the demand of increased taxes for a needless accident? Or will it be the children, in a school district beset by financial losses due to liability, who will be denied exciting activities because teachers

---

1. Bouillon v. The Harry Gill Co. and Litchfield Public School Dist. No. 12, 301 N.E.2d 627 (Ill. App. 1973).

and administrators fear recurring injuries and lawsuits? Perhaps the child who is permanently injured will pay the greatest price as he faces a future filled with pain and suffering.

In reality, it may be that all of these individuals pay the price for negligence. For these reasons, those responsible for the conduct of physical education need to understand the legal parameters of negligence and liability since negligence in the performance of a duty is the basis for most litigation.

Three cases illustrate the variety of lawsuits and the size of awards that confront the physical educator.

Lowry Stehn, an eighth grade boy, received crippling injuries during a wrestling match that was part of the required physical education program.[2] A jury returned a verdict in favor of the paralyzed boy for $385,000 reportedly the largest award by a federal court in Nashville in more than a decade.

Kelly Niles, an eleven-year-old boy, was struck on the head by a bat during a playground fight.[3] The playground supervisor was inside the school building when the fight broke out. Kelly's father took him to the hospital where two nurses, an intern and a pediatric resident examined him. Through an error at the hospital, Kelly was denied admission and sent home.

Several hours after he returned home, the boy was rushed back to the hospital for extensive brain surgery. He is now totally disabled, paralyzed from the neck down and mute. Although he has an alert mind, the brain

2. Stehn v. Bernarr McFadden Foundations, Inc., 434 F.2d 811 (6th Cir. 1970).
3. Niles v. City of San Rafael, 116 Cal. Rptr. 733 (Cal. App. 1974).

damage is such that his condition can never be improved by medical or surgical treatment. A California court granted him $4,025,000 which was, at the time, the highest personal individual injury award in United States history.

Physical education accidents and subsequent lawsuits are not restricted to the United States. In Canada, Gary Thornton attempted a somersault from a springboard but landed on his head, severely injuring his spinal cord.[4] Gary's teacher was trying to work on his report cards at the time of the accident, and also attempting to supervise activities in gymnastics, floor hockey and weight training. Gary is a permanent quadriplegic as a result of the injury.

Gary and his parents sued the teacher, the principal, and school district for negligence. He was given over $1,500,000 in damages, considered the highest personal injury award in Canadian history.

It is unfortunate that while many teachers and administrators are vulnerable to litigation, they often lack the knowledge of the elements that are essential to protect them from lawsuits. E.C. Bolmeier, a legal scholar, emphasizes that:

> Many teachers are startled to learn of their vulnerability to lawsuits arising from pupil injuries. And well they should be! If a teacher's negligence can be proved to be the proximate cause of a pupil's injury—even fatal accident, the financial damages in a judgment against the teacher could be crippling indeed. It is well, therefore, for a teacher, or anyone else, to

---

4. Thornton, Tanner et al. v. Board of Trustees of School Dist. No. 57, Edamura and Harrower, 3 W.W.R. 622 (Can. 1975).

know what constitutes 'negligence' in the eyes of the judiciary.[5]

Elements of Negligence

William Prosser, John R. Wade and Victor E. Schwartz, in *Torts, Cases and Materials*, describe four elements that must be present in a cause of action as follows:

(1) *A duty*, which is an obligation recognized by the law, requiring actor to conform to a certain standard of conduct, for the protection of others against unreasonable risks.

(2) *Breach of duty*, a failure to conform to the standard required.

(3) *Proximate or legal cause*, a reasonably close causal connection between the conduct and the resulting injury.

(4) *Damage*, actual loss resulting to the interests of another.[6]

The key to liability is the presence of negligence, since a school and its staff owe their students the duty of care that is required to save them from foreseeable harm.
Harry Rosenfield, an expert in school law, describes negligence as the "failure to act as a reasonably prudent person would act under the particular circumstances."[7]

---

5. E.C. Bolmeier, Teachers Legal Rights, Restraints and Liabilities, W.H. Anderson Co., Cincinnati, Ohio 1971.

6. William L. Prosser, John W. Wade and Victor E. Schwartz, Torts, Cases and Materials, 6th Edition Foundation Press, 1976.

7. Harry Rosenfield, Legal Liability for School Accidents, Remarks delivered at the National Conference on Accident Prevention in Physical Education, Athletics and Recreation, Washington, D.C. 1963.

Rosenfield cautions those who conduct a physical education program that:

> A liability suit presents this critical question: Could or should the teacher, in the exercise of reasonable prudence and foresight, have anticipated danger under the particular circumstances? If the answer is "Yes", the teacher is negligent if he failed to act so as to avoid such foreseeable danger or harm.[8]

Still others in the field of tort law refer to negligence as characterized by one of three elements: malfeasance (committing an unlawful act), misfeasance (improper performance of a lawful act), and nonfeasance (failure to perform a required act). While this may be an oversimplification of negligence, it does clarify an otherwise complex problem.

Malfeasance occurred in Pennsylvania when two teachers immersed a ten-year-old boy's hand in scalding water despite his protests.[9] The boy's finger was infected but it did not require emergency treatment. The boy was hospitalized for burns for twenty-eight days. The court returned a verdict of guilty against the teachers for negligence and said "any prudent person would have foreseen the scalding water aggravated the infection and permanently disfigured the boy's hand."

A boy became exhausted while running wind sprints at the end of practice on a hot and humid day.[10] The coaches administered first aid in a negligent and untrained manner and the boy died. The court ruled in favor of the

---

8. *Id.*
9. Guerrieri v. Tyson, 24 A.2d 468 (Pa. 1942).
10. Mogabgab v. Orleans Parish School Bd., 239 So. 2d 456 (La. App. 1970).

boy's parents because it felt that the improper treatment that caused the boy's death was misfeasance.

Nonfeasance could be said to occur if a student ran through a glass door in the gymnasium, severed an artery and the teacher failed to try and stop the bleeding. Physical education teachers are expected to administer emergency first aid when a person's life is at stake and failure to attempt to help the person could result in liability.

Defenses Against Negligence.

The best defense against a claim of negligence is to prove that one of the four elements required for negligence is not present. Other defenses that can result in a "no-liability" verdict for the defendant (one against whom the suit is brought) teacher, administrator or school district include contributory negligence, comparative negligence, or assumption of risk and an Act of God.

Contributory negligence prevents a person from recovering damages if he is at fault to even the slightest degree in causing his own injury. A court will consider what standard of conduct is required for someone of the person's age, physical capabilities, sex and training before it makes a decision as to fault.

One Arizona case involved the contention on the part of the defendant that the plaintiff (one who sues another and who seeks a remedy in court for injury) contributed to the injury by his negligent action.[11] Gerald Bryant was a student at Thunderbird Academy and he testified that the Dean of Boys recruited some of the students to gather pecans as a money-making project for the "Boys

11. Bryant v. Thunderbird Academy, 439 P.2d 818 (Ariz. 1968).

Club." The Dean directed Gerald to climb a tree so he could shake some pecans down. The boy broke his leg when a limb gave way and he fell to the ground.

The Supreme Court of Arizona considered the question of the size of the limb on which the boy stood prior to his fall. It reaffirmed the principle that a defendant has the burden to establish that contributory negligence existed in a personal injury action. It commented also that the "test for existence of contributory negligence is whether, in light of existing dangers, one is exercising ordinary care for his own safety."

The Arizona court reasoned that the boy had to realize the dangers of his action in climbing the tree and that this action contributed to the injury. It therefore ruled in favor of the Thunderbird Academy and denied the student any damages.

Comparative negligence means that the fault for a given circumstance is prorated. If a person is guilty of contributory negligence, it is often impossible for the plaintiff to get a favorable verdict. George Peters, a products liability attorney in California comments that most states are concerned that an injured party cannot recover damages because that party was negligent in some degree. Peters predicts that many state legislatures will follow the example of California and pass legislation permitting the use of the comparative negligence concept.[12] Some states, such as California and Virginia, now permit an individual who is partially at fault to receive compensation on a prorated basis.

Peters illustrates this by a recent case at Occidental

------

12. George Peters, Lecture delivered at the Second National Conference on Sports Safety, Chicago, Illinois, October, 1976.

College in California. A student was injured when he stepped on a loose basketball and crashed into an unpadded gymnasium wall during "free play" or intramurals. The court found the college 75 percent at fault and the student 25 percent negligent. Under comparative negligence legislation, the student, while negligent, still collected $15,000 in damages for his injury, while he would have received $45,000 had he not been at all negligent.

Assumption of risk occurs when a person assumes the responsibility for his own safety. The courts seem to distinguish clearly between physical education and athletic-related injuries when assumption of risk is the basis of a defendant's claim. The court is reluctant to uphold this defense in physical education since students are participating in required activities, whereas athletics are voluntary.

In *Teachers and Torts,* Ruth and Kern Alexander explain the rationale behind the theory of assumption of risk by pointing out that:

> The theory here is that the plaintiff in some manner consents to relieve the defendant of his duty or obligation of conduct. In other words, the plaintiff by expressed or implied agreement assumes the risk of danger and thereby relieves the defendant of responsibility. The defendant is simply not under any legal duty to protect the plaintiff. The plaintiff with knowledge of the danger voluntarily enters into a relationship with the defendants, and by doing so agrees to take his own chances.[13]

13. Ruth Alexander and Kern Alexander, Teachers and Torts, Maxwell Publishing Co., Middletown, Kentucky.

The Alexanders conclude that:

> Essential to the doctrine of assumption of risk
> is that the plaintiff have knowledge of the
> risks; if he is ignorant of the conditions and
> dangers, he does not assume the risk. If he does
> not take reasonable precautions to determine
> the hazards involved, then he has not assumed
> the risk but he may be contributorily negligent
> instead.[14]

Ralph Ruggerio, a senior in high school took off his
glasses and coat and threatened a fellow student, causing
a fight, while his teacher was in an office near the locker
room.[15] Ruggerio was injured in the fight and sued the
Board of Education in New York for failing to provide
supervision in the locker room. Testimony during the
trial revealed that the teacher was in close proximity to
the locker room and, if needed, could have prevented the
confrontation. The court of appeals reversed the lower
court's decision in favor of the plaintiff, by ruling that
the boy assumed the risk, knowing the potential consequences of his action, and therefore could not recover
damages.

An *Act of God,* sometimes referred to as an Act of
Nature, is something that occurs which is beyond the
ability of a teacher or other school authority to control. If
a group of children were in a swimming pool on a clear,
sunny day and a violent bolt of lightning struck someone
in the pool, the injury could be attributed to an unforeseen
and unexpected Act of God.

---

14. *Id.*
15. Ruggerio v. Board of Educ. of City of Jamestown, 309 N.Y.S.2d
    596 (N.Y. 1970).

Negligence: A Question for the Jury

In court cases in which negligence is alleged, ordinary questions of fact are left for a jury to decide. In *Bouillon v. The Harry Gill Co.*[16] the court made an interesting observation regarding the determination of negligence when it said:

> The right of trial by jury is recognized in the Magna Charta, our Declaration of Independence and both our State and Federal Constitutions. It is a fundamental right in our democratic judicial system. Questions which are composed of such qualities sufficient to cause reasonable men to arrive at different results should never be determined as matters of law. The debatable quality of issues such as negligence and proximate cause, the fact that fair minded men might reach different conclusions emphasizes the appropriateness and necessity of leaving such questions to a fact-finding body. The jury is the tribunal under our legal system to decide that type of issue. To withdraw such questions from the jury is to usurp its function.

Criteria for Determining Negligence Awards

Damages, in the form of astronomical awards, continue to increase each year. P.K. Peterson, an insurance executive, notes that:

> the former limits for which liability policies were written are no longer .regarded as adequate. Courts are taking judicial notice of dollar depreciation, and verdicts that would have been considered excessive ten years ago

---

16. *Supra* note 1.

are no longer regarded as sufficient to compensate an injured person for loss sustained as the result of an injury.[17]

Robin Forbes, an outstanding player at East Tennessee State University, signed a professional contract with the Cleveland Browns. Forbes had to make the team to be compensated.[18] Forbes was injured when an automobile driven by him collided with a railway engine in Johnson City, Tennessee. He sued the railroad for damages that included surgery for a herniated disc and the fact that he could no longer play football. He testified that the accident left him physically impaired.

During the trial, in which Forbes was granted $75,000, the Court of Appeals of Tennessee defined the various considerations it makes in determining the amount of damages when it said:

> the measure of damages for personal injuries is not the loss of time or earnings but the loss or impairment of ability to earn.

The court then gave a complete account of the various factors that affect an award. It listed them as follows:

> Character of plaintiff's ordinary pursuits, extent to which the injury has prevented or will prevent him from following such pursuits . . . age, health, character, capability, ability to work, intelligence, skill, talents, experience, training, industry, habits, and other personal qualities, surroundings, record of employment, station and expectancy of life, occupation, ef-

---

17. P.K. Peterson, Modern Approaches to Liability and Insurance, Proceedings of the Third Annual NACDA Convention, Cleveland, Ohio, June, 1968 at 50.
18. Clinchfield R.R. Co. v. Forbes, 417 S.W.2d 210 (Tenn. 1967).

fect of injury thereon, value of services, occupations open, and physical capacity to work when injured and thereafter.

The court stated that it could consider all factors regarding the victim's earning capacity and give each part the proper weight. It concluded:

> courts must take into consideration the nature and extent of injuries, suffering, expenses, diminution of earning capacity, inflation and high cost of living, age, life expectancy and amounts awarded in similar cases in determining whether awards for personal injuries are too high.[19]

It is interesting to look at the actual breakdown of an award for negligence. The *Thornton* case in Canada, in which a boy fell from a springboard and became a permanent quadriplegic, is divided into four categories:[20]

Special Damages	$ 42,128.87
Cost of Future Care	1,188,071.80
Loss of Ability to Earn Income	103,858.26
Loss of Amenities and Enjoyment of Life	200,000.00
	$1,534,058.93

In commenting on the award, the Canadian court emphasized that:

> the principle of law is that the victim of someone else's negligence should be put back into the position both in terms of finances and health that he would have been had he not been injured. Perfect compensation cannot be awarded, but the judge 'endeavored to use the wrongdoer's money to provide Gary with

19. *Id.*
20. *Supra* note 4.

the dignity, comfort and length of life to which we all in this society feel so rightly entitled.' [21]

In *Niles v. City of San Rafael*, in which a boy was struck by a bat in a playground fight, the California Court of Appeals denied the defendant's charge that the award was excessive. It listed the parts of the award as follows:

Lost Earnings	$ 503,570.00
Past Medical Expenses	86,240.00
Future Medical Expenses	196,902.00
Cost of Medical Supplies and Equipment	41,637.00
Medical Emergency Fund	50,000.00
Tutoring and Instruction	242,643.00
Attendant Care	1,299,637.00
Total Economic Loss	2,420,629.00
General Damages	1,604,371.00
Total	$4,025,000.00 [22]

Occasionally a large award will be judged excessive and reduced. The rationale may best be explained by a New Jersey case in which the judge lowered the $1,216,000 award to $335,140.[23] The judge sympathized with the injured boy but explained that the award was to compensate him for his past and present suffering rather than to enrich him. The judge discussed his reasoning on awards by stating:

Let's look at it another way. If the award of $1,180,000 was invested after the payment of

21. *Supra* note 4.
22. *Supra* note 3.
23. Miller v. Cloidt and the Bd. of Educ. of Borough of Catham, Docket No. L7241-62 (N.J. Super. 1964).

counsel fees, what would it return per year? Let's assume one—third would go for counsel fees and expenses or better than $787,000 would be left, at three percent the income would be $23,633.00 per year. Could not careful management of the fund increase the principal? The net result would be that Stanley could live a normal life and leave an estate more than he received for his injuries.

If present trends continue, negligent conduct will be followed by increased litigation and larger awards than ever in future years. Courts will have no mathematical formula to guide them in computing damages but will depend on many factors to remedy the suffering and loss of income that comes with serious injuries.

Summary

Students are injured more frequently in physical education accidents than in any other school-related activity. Teachers and administrators often lack the knowledge that is essential to protect them from lawsuits. The actual key to liability is the presence of negligence. For a cause of action to be valid, four elements must be present. These include a duty owed to an individual and a breach of this duty; there must be a proximate cause between the conduct of an act and the resulting injury and a loss to the interest of another must occur in the form of damage.

The best defense against a claim of negligence is to prove that one of the four elements required for negligence is not present. Other defenses that can result in a "no-liability" verdict for the defendant include contributory negligence, comparative negligence, assumption of risk and an Act of God.

In court cases in which negligence is alleged, questions of fact are left for a jury to decide. The right of trial by jury is a fundamental right in our democratic judicial system. The fact that reasonable men might reach different conclusions emphasizes the necessity for leaving such questions to a fact-finding body.

Many factors are considered in an award such as the nature and extent of the injury, suffering, expenses, diminution of earning capacity, life expectancy, the high cost of living and awards in similar cases. Perfect compensation is not possible but the principle of law is that the victim of another's negligence should be restored to health and finances in so far as possible. There is no mathematical formula to guide a court in computing damages but if trends continue negligence will be followed by increased litigation and larger awards than ever.

2. Who is Responsible for Negligence?

*Liability is a present threat, but only to those who
fail to recognize their new legal obligations and
fail to take reasonable steps to safeguard the
health and safety of those who rely on them.*[1]

One possible explanation for the rise in liability cases
may be found in the new, broader concept of physical
education. Educators now accept the fact that the school
should foster the social and physical, as well as the
academic, needs of the individual. The old idea that
physical education consisted of formal exercises has
yielded to a changing program viewed as serving the
individual throughout his life.

The desire for life-time sports in today's curriculum
has encouraged administrators to emphasize body-con-
ditioning sports such as wrestling, gymnastics and weight
training in addition to leisure-time activities such as
golfing, swimming and tennis. Title IX (20 U.S.C. § 1681
et seq.) regulations have influenced the introduction of
coeducation classes in physical education. In addition,
physical education programs are now characterized by
mini-courses, off-campus independent activities and other
innovations.

All these programs, with trampolines, springboards,
swimming pools and other equipment, are exciting for
the participants but they create a multitude of problems

---

1. George Peters, Liability in Informal Sports and Recreational
   Programs, Proceedings of the Second National Conference on
   Sports Safety, Chicago, Illinois, 1976.

for the teacher, principal and school board. The innovative activities and potentially dangerous equipment present unusual risks and hazards that require close supervision, better instruction and periodic inspection of equipment and facilities.

While it is important for school people to avoid litigation it is even more imperative that our children enjoy the protection of a safe school environment. The playing field and gymnasium must be just as safe for our children as is the classroom in which academic subjects are taught.

George Peters, speaking at the National Conference on Sports Safety, admonishes school authorities to keep in mind that:

> liability in informal sports and recreation should not be just another remote incidental concern or a topic of complaint and argument by those whose complacency may seem threatened. Liability is a present threat, but only to those who fail to recognize their new legal obligations and fail to take reasonable steps to safeguard the health and safety of those who rely on them.[2]

In most cases that go to court, the plaintiffs name as many people as possible as defendants. They usually sue the teacher, the principal, the school district and the school board in the hope someone will be judged negligent and be subject to damages. Therefore we must examine the position of each person, or class of persons frequently accused of negligence.

---

2. *Id.*

Liability of the Teacher

The American law of negligence is not to be found in a written code. It is based upon precedent or upon established modes of legal procedure. A previous judicial decision is used as a basis for subsequent decisions. Negligence is to be viewed against this background.

The fact that an accident occurs does not necessarily mean the teacher is liable for damages. It must be proved that the injury is proximately caused by the teacher's negligence.

The same standards apply to teachers regarding negligence as to private individuals. Among these are foreseeability and proximate cause. In like manner, the same defenses against negligence used by all defendants are available to teachers.

Liability, as it relates to teachers, involves an interesting contradiction. Bolmeier cautions teachers that "there are more liability suits against teachers than any others of the professional staff." He explains that this is due not to discrimination but to the fact that "they make up the greatest number of the professional staff and they are in direct contact with the pupils." [3] David Martin, a school law authority, agrees that teachers may be sued in tort actions because "they offer the only legal source of remedy for the alleged wrong." [4]

Yet Paul Proehl, an authority on tort law, describes

3. E.C. Bolmeier, Teachers' Legal Rights, Restraints and Liabilities, W.H. Anderson Co., Cincinnati, Ohio, 1971.
4. Proceedings of the Second Appalachian State Teachers College School Law Conference, Boone, N.C., Appalachian State Teachers College, 1963; hereinafter cited as Appalachian Proceedings.

teachers as "judgment-proof." [5] He writes that few people sue teachers, not because of sympathy or compassion for them, but simply because they rarely win a verdict against teachers. Even if a verdict is favorable, teachers do not possess enough money to pay for large injury awards. Proehl illustrates this "can't win" attitude by an Oklahoma case in which a student was injured during horseplay in class.[6] The teacher failed to report to class and the unsupervised students engaged in rowdy conduct. The injured student chose to sue six minor classmates rather than the teacher because she felt her chances of recovery were better served.

Proehl makes an interesting observation regarding the conduct of laymen toward certain professions when he says:

> There is much conduct in certain professions which seem a mystery to the layman (including the judge) simply because it is beyond the scope of his knowledge or comprehension. The inability of the layman to probe, to know, and to evaluate the conduct of this kind may indeed result in a greater margin of error unless the conduct is policed by the profession itself.[7]

He continues by discussing the teacher's dilemma:

> the teacher when judged by these standards is woefully lacking in protection against law suits. For example, few laymen feel inadequate or ignorant of teaching but in too many

5. Paul Proehl, *Tort Liability of Teachers*, 12 Vanderbilt L. Rev. 739 (1959).
6. Keel v. Hainline, 331 P.2d 397 (Okla. 1958).
7. Proehl, *Tort Liability of Teachers*, *supra* note 5 at 753.

instances, teachers are subjected to nonprofessional advice, interference and second guessing.

The law prohibits careless action, whatever it is. It is possible, however, for a teacher to exercise reasonable care and still be liable for negligence. In such an instance, negligence is inherent in the act. For example, how many teachers have "recruited" a volunteer to climb a high ladder in the gymnasium to replace a light bulb or directed a student to stand and mark the flight of a dangerous discus, javelin or shotput by another pupil? How many times have teachers compelled students to demonstrate an intricate gynmnastic maneuver or to dive into the deep end of a pool to retrieve some lost object? In these familiar situations the teacher may exercise reasonable care, skill and preparation but the action itself is potentially dangerous.

In other circumstances the act may become unsafe through lack of care, skill, preparation or warning although the act itself would not have ordinarily constituted negligent conduct. The failure of a teacher to warn a young boy of the danger that existed on a playground resulted in a verdict against an Illinois teacher in the amount of $40,000.[8] The physical education teacher was inside the building at the time of the accident and had assigned a seventeen-year-old boy to supervise the area. Several fast pitch games were going on near a group of very young children. A baseball bat slipped out of a player's hands and struck eight-year-old Sonny Stanley. The court found the teacher liable for his negligent

---

8. Stanley v. Board of Educ. of City of Chicago, 293 N.E.2d 417 (Ill. App. 1973).

conduct in failing to warn the participants of the risks
that were present on the crowded playground.

There are no sure criteria for determining what is
negligent action and what is not since each case stands
individually on its own merit. There are, however, certain
conditions that are likely to cause a teacher to be judged
negligent should an accident take place.

One test for determining liability is called foreseeability.
A person is liable for negligent conduct if he could have
foreseen the harmful consequences of his act yet disregards
them. No liability will be found if a teacher is judged to
have been unable to foresee such consequences.

The parents of a thirteen-year-old girl who was found
floating in a river, stabbed to death, sued her teacher for
negligence.[9] The girl left her coat, purse and textbooks
on her desk before class began and disappeared. The
teacher noticed the girl's absence but did not foresee any
problem. The parents argued that the teacher should
have foreseen the danger that could have existed and
notified school authorities. During the emotional trial it
was said:

> The mere fact that an accident happened in
> which a pupil was injured does not render the
> teacher liable.

In upholding the teacher, the Mississippi Supreme
Court concluded that the teacher was not guilty of any
negligence and that:

> A number of cases have taken the position
> that supervisory personnel were required to act

---

9. Levandoski v. Jackson County School Dist., 328 So. 2d 339
   (Miss. 1976).

to prevent an injury only where the specific-type injury was foreseeable.

A common breach of duty on the part of many teachers is absence from the classroom or playground. The Minnesota Supreme Court awarded a girl $50,000 when a fellow student hit her in the eye.[10] Since the teacher was inside the building during the accident, the court reasoned that the presence of the teacher would have prevented the rowdyism that caused the accident and found him guilty of negligence.

Alexander Christofides was stabbed in the hand by another student during an unsupervised class period.[11] The teacher failed to appear for over 25 minutes. During the trial, the testimony centered around the boy's inability to continue his piano lessons. The Court, perhaps with "tongue in cheek" questioned:

> how well he played before the injury and whether a budding genius was nipped in the bud.

It then made an interesting comment as it granted the boy $1,500 for pain and suffering and his father $100 for medical bills:

> In evaluating the damages the court cannot grant any allowance for the fact that his desire to continue with the piano lessons was weaker than his love for the piano.

It concluded:

> While there appears to be no great burning desire to continue his piano playing, let us hope

---

10. Sheehan v. Saint Peter's Catholic School, 188 N.W.2d 868 (Minn. 1971).
11. Christofides v. Hellenic Eastern Orthodox Christian Church of New York, 227 N.Y.S.2d 946 (N.Y. Mun. Ct. 1962).

that if any spark is left it will be rekindled before he is ninety so that his parents might reap the pleasure.

A second test for determining liability is called proximate cause. A teacher may be liable if the negligence is proved to be the proximate cause of the injury.

William Brod came to physical education class without his gym shoes and reported that his teacher told him to play in his bare feet if he wanted to participate with his classmates.[12] The boy testified that his feet stuck to the floor, causing him to trip and fall and injure his front teeth. The Supreme Court, Rensselaer County, felt that the physical education teacher's conduct in directing the boy to play in bare feet was the proximate cause of the injury. It, therefore, awarded the boy $15,000 and an additional $3,800 to his father.

Douglas Coates, a student in the state of Washington, was a member of a school-sanctioned extra-curricular activity.[13] Although the club met off campus and it was reported that drinking often took place, the school did not furnish a teacher to supervise the meetings. Coates was involved in an automobile accident on the way home from a Saturday night meeting at 2:00 a.m. His parents sued the school for failing to meet its obligation by furnishing a supervisor.

The Supreme Court of Washington did not agree with the allegations and ruled that the absence of a supervisor was not the proximate cause of the injury since the

---

12. Brod v. Central School Dist. No. 1, Rensselaer County, 386 N.Y.S.2d 125, 53 A.D. 2d 1002 (N.Y. App. Div. 1976).
13. Coates v. Tacoma School Dist. No. 10, 347 P.2d 1093 (Wash. 1960), ch. 2, n. 13.

school did not require organizations meeting off campus to have a supervisor present.

It is obvious that teachers will continue to be sued as long as injuries take place. Bolmeier, however, reassures all teachers when he concludes that in the majority of cases in which teachers were charged with negligence, the court favored them. "In fact," he comments, "no court has held a defendant liable where there was substantial evidence that the defendant acted with prudence and caution in the performance of his duties."[14]

Liability of the Administrator

Administrators (superintendents and principals) are named as defendants less frequently than are other individuals. Martin explains that this "lack of litigation is no doubt due largely to the fact that the school administrator is generally one step removed from direct contact with pupils."[15] Also, administrators are at times considered to be officers of the state with accompanying immunity. However, they are usually treated as school employees and have little reason to be complacent in regard to liability for their own negligence and that of their subordinates. Administrators, like teachers, are liable under the general principles of tort law for their own personal acts of negligence and wrongdoing.[16]

Administrators have been sued for a variety of reasons but in tort actions the majority of cases involve rules and regulations, instruction, equipment and facilities, super-

---

14. Bolmeier, *supra* note 3 at 129.
15. APPALACHIAN PROCEEDINGS at 21.
16. *Who is Liable for Pupil Injuries?* (Washington, D.C. NEA, 1963) at 29.

vision, due process and the overall operation of the school. Several cases illustrate the type of litigations that involve administrators.

Ten students in Indiana, elected to remain inside the classroom to work on an assignment instead of going outside to play during an open recess period.[17] The teacher left the group unsupervised and went outside the immediate area. William Miller opened another student's tackle box in search of a pencil. The box contained a battery and a detonator cap that looked like a Christmas bulb to the boy. He touched the cap to the battery and it exploded, permanently damaging his eye.

The injured student sued the principal for having a rule that permitted a teacher to leave a class unsupervised. The principal admitted that he had formulated a rule that enabled a teacher to have free time during the recess period. The rule allowed a teacher to consider all facets of the situation and, if convinced that the circumstances permitted, to leave the students in the classroom alone. The principal furnished supervision for the open recess on the playground.

The teacher, in the present case, testified that the students were eager to work on their assignment and that no problem children were present in the room. In addition she asked the teacher in the adjoining room to look in on the group from time to time.

Two questions were raised during the trial:

(1) Was the principal's rule reasonable?
(2) Was the action of the teacher discretionary (a duty requiring the exercise of judgment) or ministerial (a duty which a public officer is required by law to perform)?

---

17. Miller v. Griesel, 297 N.E.2d 463 (Ind. App. 1973).

The court considered the teacher's act to be discretionary and free from liability and the principal's rule reasonable. It, therefore, dismissed the case against him.

David Flournoy, a student in Colorado, and several classmates in physical education attempted to cross a busy street from the gymnasium to the playground.[18] Flournoy ran into a speeding car and died from the injuries he sustained.

His parents charged the superintendent and principal with negligent conduct for failing to adopt rules that would provide a safe crossing for the student. They contended that the crossing was dangerous because of the heavy traffic and needed safeguards.

In Colorado, public officials are charged with negligence under the doctrine of *respondeat superior* (imposes liability on an employer for the acts of his employee) when:

> they fail to use ordinary care, therein, or, where they have been negligent in supervising the acts of their subordinates or have directed or authorized the wrong.[19]

The court stated that public officials are not expected to be held liable for honest mistakes, but on the other hand, they cannot avoid their obligation to the public by failing to fulfill their duties.

The administrators argued that their acts were not the proximate cause of the accident and that they could not have prevented his death by anything they could have done. The district court returned a verdict in favor of the defendants and the plaintiffs appealed. The Supreme Court of Colorado reversed the original decision of the

18. Flournoy v. McComas, 488 P.2d 1104 (Colo. 1971).
19. Liber v. Flor, 415 P.2d 332 (Colo. 1966).

defendants and remanded the case back to a jury for determination of the facts.

One of the judges dissented by pointing out that the administrators did not select the site or control the location of the playground. He felt that they were not guilty of negligence. It is reported that the case was retried and the court ruled in favor of the defendant superintendent and principal.

The courts have considered several cases in which an inherently dangerous condition was not corrected and a student was injured. In a Michigan case,[20] a child was injured on the school playground when her sled hit a steel post. The girl's father sued for $60,000 and argued vehemently that the school authorities had sufficient knowledge of the dangerous situation but failed to correct it in a reasonable time. He stressed the fact that numerous accidents had resulted from the location of the steel post but that the school officials had continued to ignore it. The court found no breach of duty against the principal and upheld the district's claim of immunity.

The court reacted differently in Washington, D.C. however, when a young boy wandered through a hole in a chain fence on the playground.[21] The boy strayed into a busy street, became confused and was hit by a car and killed as he tried to get back to the playground. The boy's parents sued the school charging the principal with negligence for failing to have the fence repaired. The court ruled that the duty to repair the fence was ministerial and not protected by governmental immunity. The ques-

---

20. Stevens v. City of St. Clair Shores, 115 N.W.2d 69 (Mich. 1962).
21. Ballard v. Polly, 387 F. Supp. 895 (D.C. Cir. 1975).

tion was asked "how far does a school have to go to insure the safety of its students?" The court answered that while the school is not an absolute insurer of its students it does owe a duty to protect its students from the hazard of the street. It considered the gap in the fence, the school's knowledge of its existence, the age of the deceased, the proximity of the busy intersection to the school and then ruled that the defendant was guilty of negligence for failing to correct the dangerous condition that existed.

In another case a New York court ruled that a warning of danger is all that is necessary on the part of a principal.[22] No one was supervising the playground when a boy slipped on a fence on the school grounds. The principal provided supervision in the lunch room but not on the playground at noontime. On the day in question, the boy was given permission by his teacher to play outside after lunch.

The principal reminded the court that he had made periodic warnings to all his pupils about the fence from which the boy fell. The boy admitted that he had received several warnings about the fence but that he had deliberately ignored them. The Education Code stated that a warning about the fence was sufficient to provide adequate supervision for the pupils in the school. The court, therefore, concluded that the boy was guilty of contributory negligence and dismissed the case against the principal.

---

22. Schuyler v. Board of Educ. of Union Free School Dist. No. 7, 239 N.Y.S.2d 769 (N.Y. App. Div. 1963).

Liability of the School District

The common-law principle which protects school districts with immunity is used as a defense by school districts without regard to the circumstances of the case in question.

An example of this is the case of Lisa Haney who was injured in a school bus accident in North Carolina. As a result of the injury, Lisa is paralyzed from the chest down. Her hospital bill for the first four weeks was over $5,000. Lisa's father is a disabled farmer whose only income is from a pension check for $168 per month. North Carolina law permits a payment under the Tort Claims Act of $600 for an accident on a school bus. As a consequence, Lisa and her parents face an almost impossible situation. Through no fault of Lisa's she will face a limited life because of her paralyzed condition, with no way to pay the medical bills.[23]

Lisa's friends are conducting a massive billboard campaign throughout the state to call attention to her dilemma. Billboards featuring her picture carry the caption "Tell Lisa it was no one's fault." Friends hope the campaign will influence North Carolina legislators to liberalize the insurance coverage for future school bus accidents.[24]

Harry Rosenfield, an opponent of sovereign and governmental immunity, decries an outmoded doctrine that places injured students in an unfair position such as the one confronting Lisa Haney. Rosenfield expresses

---

23. Greensboro Daily News, January 16, 1977.
24. *Id.*

his opposition to the immunity doctrine by protesting that:

> The present rule, in my judgment, is completely inconsistent with all modern concepts of justice and social responsibility. It is unreasonable to require an injured person to bear a disproportionate part of the normal operating cost of activities undertaken by the entire community.[25]

Rosenfield continues his dissent by pointing out that:

> The whole community pays for the school building, for light, heat, books, school contracts, etc. Why should the injured pupil or teacher pay out of his own pocket for an item that is an operating cost of the school budget— in fact, if not in law. If the school breaks a contract, it is liable in law. If it breaks someone's neck, it is not. I submit that this does not make sense.[26]

When school districts are sued for negligence, the terms common law, sovereign immunity, governmental immunity and charitable immunity are frequently used. Common law refers to the laws that have been established by the English Parliament and were in effect at the time of the American Revolution. Our legislatures have enacted many laws since then but some states follow the laws peculiar to the common law when liability arises.

The school districts in such states compare to the

---

25. Rosenfield, Legal Liability for School Accidents, Remarks delivered at the National Conference on Accident Prevention in Physical Education, Athletics and Recreation, Washington, D.C. 1963.
26. *Id.* at 7.

agents of the King and enjoy immunity from torts called
"sovereign immunity" for the states and "governmental
immunity" for political subdivisions of the state, such as
cities, counties and school districts. James Palmer, a
Kansas City attorney, distinguishes between the two but
observes that courts often do not. Since the two immunity
doctrines are theoretically distinct, it is possible for a
state to have one and not the other. Charitable immunity
is analagous to sovereign and governmental immunity
but deals with private institutions rather than public
ones.[27]

Palmer comments that immunity is changing rapidly
and therefore it is difficult to assess the status of immunity
from state to state. He lists several categories that exist
in various states:

> (1) governmental—proprietary (when a govern-
>   mental agency engages in a profit-making
>   business). Activities that are govern-
>   mental are immune from torts while pro-
>   prietary acts are not.
> (2) Ministerial-discretionary-ministerial acts
>   are subject to suit, while discretionary
>   acts are immune from suit.

Most courts have trouble distinguishing between
governmental and proprietary activities or between
ministerial and discretionary acts. Palmer points out
that "As a result certain activities will vary from
jurisdiction to jurisdiction." [28]

Many arguments have been advanced for perpetuating

------

27. James Palmer, The Case of the Disappearing Immunities, Pro-
    ceedings of NAIA Athletic Director's Workshop, Kansas City,
    Missouri, March, 1976.
28. *Id.*

the common-law principle in tort cases involving school districts. One argument is that *stare decisis* (a Latin expression meaning that once a principle has been accepted by the court the decision stands) and stability in the law requires it. Another is that funds are not available to meet the tort claims that would be brought against the school district.

The common-law principle is used as a defense by some school districts without regard to the circumstances of the case in question. Unless a statute exists to the contrary, this principle protects the school against excessive liability suits and subsequent damages. Many school districts escape litigation because they plead immunity under the doctrine. Children receive injuries because of a lack of supervision, incompetent instruction, defective equipment, unsafe facilities and dangerous activities, but as long as the school district can claim immunity it is absolved from damages.

Two court cases illustrate the attitude of the courts toward school districts that are clothed in the immunity doctrine.

Jraquetta Scott, a second grader in Florida, went on a school picnic.[29] During the field trip, the girl fell in Snapper Creek and drowned. Her parents sued the school district alleging that their daughter drowned because there was a lack of supervision. The circuit court ruled in favor of the girl's parents but the District Court of Appeal of Florida reversed the decision by upholding the immunity doctrine of the Dade County School District.

Jeffrey Pichette was visiting friends in Manistique,

29. School Bd. of Dade County v. Scott, 313 So. 2d 50 (Fla. Dist. Ct. App. 1975).

Michigan during the summer vacation.[30] The boy went to the school playground to slide on the sliding board. The playground was unfenced and no one was present when the boy climbed up on the slide. As he came down the slide, he caught an eleven-inch sliver of wood in his thigh. Jeffrey was rushed to the hospital where he underwent emergency surgery. The local police roped the slide off immediately and dismantled it the following day.

The boy sued the school district for permitting a defective slide to stand on the playground. The trial court ruled that the school district enjoyed immunity and was not liable for its negligence and the boy appealed the decision.

The Court of Appeals of Michigan supported the lower court's decision and ruled that the district did not waive its immunity because it purchased liability insurance. It reasoned that the playground did not operate for a profit and was, therefore, not a proprietary function by nature, even though the accident took place during the summer when school was not in session.

The dissatisfaction with the doctrine continues, with various experts predicting its continuance or abolishment. The fact remains however, that only a small number of states have been willing to change the archaic common-law principle and permit injured pupils to sue the school district.

Although the number of states that have completely

---

30. Pichette v. Manistique Public Schools, 213 N.W.2d 784 (Mich. App. 1973).

abrogated the immunity doctrine are few, Martin predicts that the trend is away from the past rule of immunity.[31]

Rosenfield sees hope for a change in the attitude of the states toward immunity when he writes that:

> The increasing efforts by courts and legislatures, and by self-insurance plans, indicate the growing realization of the fundamental inhumanity and impropriety of continuing a centuries-old rule of law which is not only archaic, but it is also unfair and unjust.[32]

Rosenfield describes the encouraging measures adopted by some states as: general waivers, indemnity statutes, safe-place statutes and school insurance. He explains that California and Hawaii, as well as a few others, have waived liability completely while Washington is liable for all school activities except for accidents that occur involving playground equipment and athletic apparatus. Some states have passed a statute that is called save-harmless or hold-harmless in which a teacher on trial for negligence is furnished a lawyer and if found guilty, the school district pays the cost of the award for the teacher. Other states authorize such payment of a judgment for a teacher but do not require it.[33]

Wisconsin is an example of states that require the school district to provide safe school premises or be liable for suits. Many states require public-owned buses

---

31. D. Martin, Trends in Tort Liability of School Districts as Revealed by Court Decisions (1962) (Unpublished Doctoral Dissertation) Duke University, Durham, N.C. at 243.
32. Rosenfield, Legal Liability for School Accidents, *supra* note 25.
33. *Id.*

to have the protection of liability insurance and others permit school boards to purchase liability insurance.[34]

Ruth and Kern Alexander point out that a school district must have authorization by statute to purchase liability insurance. They view the purchase of liability insurance as a:

> humanitarian gesture on the part of the legislature to assist children or employees who are injured in some phase of the educational program.[35]

Since the doctrines of sovereign, governmental and charitable immunity are changing rapidly it is necessary to consult the state laws, both statutes and cases, to determine the current status of these doctrines.[36] (See Appendix A for listing of the individual states' position on immunity)

Summary

Physical education is changing to a broader program of participation and activities and this increases problems of people everywhere. Innovative activities, such as contracting, and potentially dangerous equipment present unusual risks and hazards that require close supervision, better instruction and periodic inspection of equipment and facilities.

It is essential that our children enjoy the protection of a safe environment. The playing field and gymnasium

---

34. *Supra* note 25.
35. Alexander, Teachers and Torts, Maxwell Publishing Co., Middletown, Kentucky at 53.
36. Palmer, *supra* note 27 at 1.

must be just as safe for our children as is the classroom in which academic subjects are taught.

In the majority of cases that go to court, the plaintiff names as many people as possible as defendants. The fact that an accident takes place, however, does not mean that someone is liable. In fact it has been said, that no defendant has been found guilty when there was sufficient evidence that the defendant acted with caution in the performance of his duties. There are no sure criteria for determining what is negligent action and what is not since each case stands individually on its own merit.

Teachers are closer to students and are sued more often than any other party connected with the school. Teachers are bound by the same standards regarding negligence and defenses against negligence as any private citizen. While they are named as defendants in most cases, some argue that teachers are becoming "judgment-proof" since they usually do not possess enough money to pay large awards.

Administrators are named less frequently as defendants than are other individuals since they are generally one step removed from direct contact with students. At times administrators are considered officers of the state with accompanying immunity but more often they are treated as school employees and liable for their negligent acts. Administrators are sued for a variety of reasons but the majority of cases involve rules and regulations, instruction, equipment and facilities, supervision, due process and the overall operation of the school.

School districts still rely heavily on the protection of the doctrine of sovereign, governmental immunity; private schools cling to the doctrine of charitable immunity.

These districts claim that funds are not available to meet the awards of lawsuits that would be brought against them.

School law experts, however, predict that more states will abrogate the immunity doctrines in the next few years. They applaud the efforts of the courts and legislatures to establish insurance, save-harmless statutes, general waivers, safe place statutes and other remedies as humanitarian, and a recognition that the outmoded doctrines are unfair and unjust.

3. Additional Cases Involving Negligence

*In making sensitive judgment calls a teacher must
not be made aware of the precariousness of his
position, as was Damocles, beneath some
economic falchion, suspended by the
the hair of hindsight.*[1]

Since the majority of pupil injury cases in physical
education involve negligence, this chapter will review
additional cases that involve a variety of situations in
which negligence is charged. The litigation is usually
directed toward the teacher, the administrator or the
school district. In some instances it is claimed against all
three.

Although each case rests on its own merit, court
decisions do give an insight into acceptable modes of
conduct for school authorities.

This chapter will consider cases that relate to some
particular area of supervision and instruction in an
attempt to answer the numerous questions that arise.

Supervision and the Teacher

A teacher is expected to perform as a parent of ordinary
prudence would act under similar conditions. As a rule
teachers can be held liable when they fail to perform a
duty owed their students. The courts consider whether
the teacher's presence would have prevented an accident
that occurred in the teacher's absence. It considers the

---

1. Berg v. Merricks, 318 A.2d 220 (Md. App. 1974).

time, place, age and other factors, as well as the teacher's ability to anticipate danger that reasonably prudent persons would have foreseen.[2]

A. Absence of the Teacher

When a claim of negligent supervision is brought against a teacher who was absent during an accident, the court tries to determine the reason for the teacher's absence, the age and type of student left alone, and the length of the teacher's absence.[3] Let's examine several situations in which the teacher was absent from class.

Daniel Kersey, a thirteen-year-old boy in Missouri, received a severe head injury when a fellow student threw him to the floor during a class in physical education.[4] The boy's teacher was absent and another teacher attempted to look after the students in addition to his own class. The boy went to the school nurse and was allowed to return to class for further participation. Daniel became ill but was instructed to remain at school until his parents could be contacted. The boy's father came to school and took his son to a local physician. Daniel died several hours later from the head injury he received in the physical education class.

The boy's parents sued for alleged negligence that charged:

> (1) Inadequate supervision for allowing an eighth-grade class of 20-25 students to be taught by another teacher who had the respon-

---

2. McGee v. Board of Educ. of City of New York, 226 N.Y.S.2d 329 (N.Y. App. Div. 1962).
3. Cirillo v. City of Milwaukee, 150 N.W.2d 460 (Wisc. 1967).
4. Kersey v. Harbin, 531 S.W.2d 76 (Mo. App. 1975).

sibility of teaching his own class at the same
time;

(2) Failure to properly supervise the classes by
putting one class in the locker room while the
other remained unsupervised in the gymnasium;

(3) Failure to directly supervise the class when
several students were known to be trouble-
makers with a past history of fighting and agi-
tating fellow students;

(4) Allowing Daniel to resume his activities in
class after he received severe head injuries.

The defendant teacher, principal and school nurse
contended that they were performing governmental duties
and were therefore immune from liability. The teacher
argued that a relationship of *in loco parentis* (in place of
the parents) existed between him and the student and as
such exonerated him from liability "for an unintentional
tort, as none was committed."[5]

The Missouri Court of Appeals heard the testimony
and made an interesting comment. It stated that there is
no general principle that guarantees immunity to teachers
for negligence and that even if the doctrine of *in loco
parentis* was still valid, it does not permit a teacher to be
negligent.

The Missouri court reasoned however, that there was
no evidence furnished at the trial that explained if there
was due cause for the teacher's absence or whether the
principal had previous knowledge of the teacher's absence.
Later information was reported that indicated that the
teacher was directed to attend a seminar instead of
meeting with the class. The administrator did not replace

---

5. *Id.*

the teacher with a substitute but combined the class with another one.

After considering all the evidence, the court dismissed the plaintiff's appeal stating:

> We fully realize we have accomplished very little by this opinion other than to dispose of the appeal, but to reiterate, the parties have tendered us abstractions, rather than concrete propositions to be decided on specific facts, and we will state once more that [sic] an appellate court is neither a law school nor a debating society, and (its) opinion is no place for a legal monograph or matters.

It did grant, however, the opportunity to the boy's parents to amend their petition and continue to litigate the case if they chose to do so.

The plaintiff's attorneys did file an amended petition in which it furnished new evidence. The defendants argued that the new discovery was not included in the previous evidence and requested a summary judgment.

At the present time the case is pending before the court.

Paul Swaitkowski was injured when he returned to his desk and sat on a pencil point placed there by a fellow student.[6] The teacher was helping another teacher in the book room which was located ten feet from the classroom.

The boy's parents charged the teacher with a lack of supervision and accused the school board of hiring an incompetent teacher. The trial court ruled in the boy's favor but the New York Supreme Court overruled the lower court's decision. The higher court set aside the

---

6. Swaitkowski v. Board of Educ. of City of Buffalo, 319 N.Y.S.2d 783 (N.Y. App. Div. 1971).

$5,343 judgment and emphatically declared that the record showed that the teacher was competent. It made a strong point regarding a teacher's absence from class when it stated:

> In effect, respondents would impose upon the Board a duty to require a teacher to call for outside assistance during her short absence from the classroom. Upon the facts of this case, we cannot so hold. A contrary holding in the circumstances of this case would effectively impose on both a school board and teacher the standard of care akin to an insurer rather than the standard of a reasonable and prudent parent.

Donald Cirillo was injured in a Milwaukee high school when a basketball game turned into a rough game of "keep-away."[7] After calling the roll, the physical education teacher left 48 boys unsupervised to shoot basketballs for a period of 25 minutes. During the "keep-away" game, Donald was slammed to the floor and injured.

The teacher was sued on three counts:

(1) failing to provide the class with rules;
(2) attempting to teach an excessive number of students;
(3) leaving the class unattended when it was common knowledge that 48 adolescent boys would become wild and reckless.

The Supreme Court of Wisconsin took exception to the trial court's verdict in favor of the teacher and stated that a jury could find the teacher guilty of negligence for leaving the class alone for such a period of time. The

---

7. *Supra* note 3.

court felt that the presence of the teacher in the gymnasium would have prevented the rough game in which the plaintiff was injured. It, therefore, reversed the trial court's decision in behalf of the teacher and favored the injured student instead.

B. Emergencies During Class

Many teachers are faced with a dilemma when an emergency takes place during a class period. When a student is injured and needs medical attention, the teacher often leaves the class to get help.

A New Jersey case had a profound effect on teachers who are tempted to leave students unsupervised for any reason. The case represents a landmark decision and has served as a guide for teachers since 1964. Stanley Miller disregarded his teacher's warning not to use the springboard while he was out of the class for the purpose of taking an injured student for medical help.[8] Stanley jumped off the springboard and landed wrong, severely injuring himself. He is permanently paralyzed.

The Millers contended that the instructor failed to exercise reasonable supervision since the springboard was a "dangerous piece of equipment." They asserted that Stanley's teacher should have foreseen the injury that resulted.

The defendant teacher and school board replied that the fourteen-year-old junior high school boy assumed the risk of the activity when he deliberately ignored the teacher's warning not to use the equipment while he was

---

8. Miller v. Cloidt and the Bd. of Educ. of Borough of Chatham, Docket No. L7241-62 (N.J. Super. 1964).

out of the area. They also accused Stanley of contributory negligence for using the equipment and added that the plaintiff failed to prove that the teacher's conduct was the proximate cause of the injury.

The plaintiff furnished an expert in physical education who testified that the defendant teacher should have put mats near the springboard, employed a mechanical rig to assist the students with midair stunts and prohibited students from supervising the gymnastic exercises.

The defendants produced four witnesses to refute the allegations of the "expert" by stating that reasonable care was exercised in this situation. The defendants stressed the fact that everyone in the class, including Stanley Miller, knew that the equipment was dangerous. They pointed out that the students were trained as spotters and that Stanley was a good athlete with skill in performing midair somersaults.

During the trial, the New Jersey court referred to an old case in which contributory negligence was discussed. In *Daniel v. West Jersey S.R.R.*[9] the court answered several questions regarding youth and contributory negligence when it said:

> The conduct of a child should not be measured by the standard of care applied to an adult.

It added that:

> Thoughtlessness, impulsiveness and indifference to all but patent and imminent dangers are natural traits of childhood, and must be taken into account when we come to classify the conduct of the child.

---

9. Daniel v. West Jersey S.R.R., 84 N.J.L. 685 (N.J. 1937).

The New Jersey court in the *Miller* case agreed that Stanley was not guilty of contributory negligence and awarded him $1,180,000 in damages plus $35,140 to his parents for medical expenses.

Judge Elden Mills later reduced the award to $335,140 when both parties agreed not to appeal the decision to a higher court.

It seems that the school district was anxious to settle for a lesser award while the parents were afraid that the award could be reduced even more in a higher court. Both parties, therefore, agreed to the award.

Many teachers who previously left their classes unattended now consider the type of equipment and activity in the class before they leave. In emergencies many teachers now send for help and stay with their classes if dangerous equipment or activities are involved.

C. Inadequate Supervision

Stanley Passafaro testified that he came to class without his gym shoes.[10] He claimed that his teacher directed him to take off his street shoes and participate in the tumbling activity in his socks. Stanley testified that he was injured when he lost his footing as he was about to jump on the mat and fell on the floor.

His physical education teacher agreed that it would be unwise to participate in such an activity in stocking feet but testified that he did not give the boy permission to take part in the activity. He did, in fact, direct him to

---

10. Passafaro v. Board of Educ. of City of New York, 353 N.Y.S.2d 178 (N.Y. App. Div. 1974).

stand on the sidelines and observe the activity but the boy ignored him and took part anyway.

The court instructed the jury to decide the case on two points:

(1) improper instruction to exercise in stocking feet;
(2) failure to provide adequate or sufficient supervision.

The Supreme Court of New York County commented that supervision could not have prevented the boy's action and subsequent injury. It ruled that the teacher was not guilty of negligence.

Pamela Brackman was struck in the face by a bat thrown by another student in a softball game in Tennessee and required extensive dental surgery as a result of the accident.[11] At the time of the incident Pamela, the captain of her softball team, was catching behind the bat without a catcher's mask. The teacher who was named as a defendant in the lawsuit did not assign the students positions on the field but left the choice to the individual students. A student at bat hit the ball and, as she ran toward first base, threw the bat which hit the plaintiff.

Pamela, the injured plaintiff, claimed that her injuries were caused by the teacher's failure to provide adequate supervision. As a second charge, she contended that the teacher failed to provide her with a protective catcher's mask.

The teacher answered the allegations by attributing the girl's injury to the throwing of the softball bat by

---

11. Brackman v. Adrian, 472 S.W.2d 735 (Tenn. App. 1971).

another student. She added that Pamela had assumed the risk of injury by choosing to catch behind the bat. She reported that the school supplied a catcher's mask but left the decision to wear it up to the students. The teacher testified that she was standing in the center of the field so she could watch the girls' game and also a game of softball played by the boys.

The Court of Appeals of Tennessee decided that the evidence did not support actionable negligence against the teacher nor did the girl's failure to wear the mask constitute negligence on the part of the teacher. The court held that Pamela had passed her fourteenth birthday and therefore could be found guilty of contributory negligence. It reversed the lower court's decision in favor of the girl and ruled instead that the teacher was in no way guilty of negligence.

Michael Berg, a senior at Crossland Senior High School in Maryland, fractured his neck during a gymnastic exercise on the trampoline.[12] As a result of the injury, Michael is a paraplegic and permanently disabled.

Michael and his mother sued the physical education teacher, the principal and superintendent, and the school board for negligence. The plaintiffs charged the defendants with negligence for failing to furnish adequate and competent supervision, failure to use a trampoline frame to insure safe performance by the students and the failure of the teacher to keep records of each student's progress.

The testimony furnished at the trial revealed that the teacher was qualified in gymnastics. He majored in

---

12. *Supra* note 1.

physical education at Maryland University and had qualilfied as a finalist in the intramural trampoline competition at the University. He taught trampolining at Gallaudet College for the Deaf while a student at the University and later taught it at a junior high school and several elementary schools.

The plaintiffs quoted from the *Segerman v. Jones* case in which it was said:

> Parents do not send their children to school to be returned to them maimed because of the absence of proper supervision.[13]

The Court of Appeals of Maryland admitted that the statement was a strong one in the face of the tragic accident in the present case but supported the position of the teacher when it declared:

> No more than doctors or lawyers should teachers be forced to perform their responsibilities with trepidation, in fear of being held accountable without knowing the standards which they are called upon to meet.[14]

The Maryland court then discussed the inherent risks of physical education when it said:

> The nature of physical education activities comprehends physical hazards. The instructor must avoid as many of these hazards as he is humanly able considering the limitations, under which he instructs, but the system cannot be made childproof.

---

13. Segerman v. Jones, 259 A.2d 794 (Md. 1969).
14. *Supra* note 1.

The Maryland court found no evidence of negligence and upheld the decision of the lower court favoring the defendants. The court made an important observation regarding the plaintiff's argument that the teacher failed to observe Michael's actions directly by stating:

> As delicate a balance exists in attempting to develop a child's body as in attempting to develop his mind. How to maintain that balance is largely a matter of judgment. To the extent that a child is given personal attention, thirty-nine others may be deprived. Which need is given preference upon a given time is a decision made hundreds of times a day by a teacher. The problems are multiplied as a teacher comes to know his students and their various needs and differences. All of these decisions occur repeatedly every fifty minutes daily with classes of various sizes.

Physical education teachers can take renewed hope from the Maryland court's attitude toward judgment calls teachers must make daily. It may well be that this court has expressed the feelings of teachers everywhere when it emphasizes that:

> In making sensitive judgment calls a teacher must not be made aware of the precariousness of his position, as was Damocles, beneath some economic falchion, suspended by the hair of hindsight. The courts are just as much a shield to a teacher who has acted prudently as they are a weapon against him if he has neglected his duty; but a jury cannot measure his actions without some measures of a professional conduct.[15]

---

15. *Supra* note 1.

Supervision and the Administrator

Administrators are required to furnish supervision for their students on the school premises. In addition they are expected to formulate rules and regulations for the safety of students and see that the rules are enforced. Once again, court decisions reveal the court's position regarding the administrators role in supervision.

A. Inadequate Supervision

A New Jersey principal was sued because he attempted to supervise the entire playground area before school began in the morning.[16] The principal admitted that he was the sole supervisor for 560 students in addition to 70 who gathered at the playground before school began and waited to be bused to another school.

A nine-year-old boy was "shot by a paper clip by a thirteen-year-old boy described as a bully." The boy was seriously injured and sued the parents of the boy who injured him, the principal and the school board.

A New Jersey court found the principal guilty of negligence for failing to assign additional personnel to the playground as supervisors. Over fifteen teachers were available to help but none were given the assignment. The plaintiff was awarded a total of $41,000 in damages. The parents of the boy who shot the paperclip paid one-half and since New Jersey has passed save-harmless legislation, the school board paid its share and that of the principal.

---

16. Titus v. Lindberg, 228 A.2d 65 (N.J. 1967).

William Ogelsby was beaten on the way home from school by a student who had been suspended earlier in the day.[17] The boy died from the injuries he received. The parents of the deceased sued the school principal for failing to provide supervision for the students at the school and particularly for their son.

The District Court of Appeals in Florida upheld the lower court's decision and dismissed the case against the principal. It ruled that the principal did not owe students who were away from the school in non-school programs a duty of supervision.

B. Failure to Formulate Rules

The father of Gordon McDonald sued a Louisiana School Board, the teacher, the principal and a ten-year-old boy, Larry, who injured his son, Gordon, in school.[18] Bad weather forced the students to go on a "rainy day" schedule which meant that the students could not go outside during the lunch recess but were required to play in their classrooms. Gordon and a boy named Larry were in a special education class. Both boys were considered to be retarded but educable. Gordon was eight months older than Larry.

The boys' teacher went to the lounge for coffee and when she did Gordon began chasing Larry and a fight erupted. Gordon chased Larry out of the classroom and Larry threatened to throw a broom at him if he did not

---

17. Ogelsby v. Seminole County Bd. of Public Instruction, 328 So. 2d 515 (Fla. Dist. Ct. App. 1976).
18. McDonald v. Terrebonne Parish School Bd., 253 So. 2d 558 (La. App. 1971).

stop coming after him. When Gordon continued to pursue Larry, the latter turned and threw a broom that struck Gordon in the eye. The injury caused Gordon to lose the sight in his eye.

The issue in the case centered around the principal's alleged failure to take precautionary measures with the students to avoid such incidents.

The Louisiana court found no fault with Larry for throwing the broom at the larger boy in self-defense. The court did not consider a common household broom to be inherently dangerous nor did it think throwing the broom constituted excessive force.

Since the teacher had requested another teacher next door to check on her class, the court did not feel the teacher was negligent just because she left her class unsupervised. It stated:

> The fact that each student is not personally supervised every moment of each school day does not constitute fault on the part of the School Board or its employees.

Evidence at the trial indicated that Larry had a record of previous incidents in which fighting took place. The school principal testified, however, that Larry was by no means the worst boy in school. He added that "this is a special education situation involving handicapped children" and to find a record of perfect conduct would be most unusual.

The Louisiana court dismissed the charge of negligence against the principal by ruling that he had not handled the situation in a negligent manner.

Supervision and the School District (School Board)

School districts that waive or modify the immunity doctrines receive the majority of cases involving school accidents.

Paul Proehl makes an interesting observation regarding the liability of the school district as opposed to that of the teacher when he writes:

> common-law jurisdictions are merely applying classic rules of negligence law against the plaintiff, as a result of which the teachers are usually exonerated, whereas the states providing a direct action against the school unit have diluted traditional negligence concepts and in many cases, despite the protestations of their courts to the contrary, tend to treat the school unit as an insurer.[19]

Since the school district is named in practically every suit involving a student injury this chapter will only consider one area of litigation to show the position of the court regarding the school district. The playground is litigated heavily and it does not seem to matter if the injury occurred before class, during class, after school or during vacation periods. Negligence is the determining factor in these cases.

As reported in *From the Gym to the Jury*[20], cases litigated before the early 1960's met with consistent decisions by the courts. When children were injured on

---

19. Paul Proehl, *Tort Liability of Teachers*, 12 Vanderbilt L. Rev. 739 (1959).
20. Herb Appenzeller, From the Gym to the Jury, Michie Company, Charlottesville, Va., 1970.

the playgrounds in non-school activities and during non-school hours, the courts held as a general rule that school authorities did not need to provide supervision. The court's rationale for this was that a playground was by far safer than the crowded streets for children at play. The courts were just as consistent in the exceptions that found negligence on the part of the school or its employees. The courts expected and even demanded safe facilities, free from hazards. When unsupervised playgrounds were not free from a defect the court invariably held the school liable. Later cases indicate that at least in this area of liability, the courts have not changed their positions from that stated above.

Joseph Orsini was struck by a bicyclist on a New York playground in 1974.[21] The eight-year-old boy was a spectator at a baseball game on the playground when he was injured by a bicyclist. The accident occurred on a Saturday and was in a non-related school activity. The New York Court found that the school district was not negligent since it had no previous knowledge that bicycles were ridden in a negligent manner on the playground. It ruled that the school district was not responsible for furnishing supervision.

In New York a seven-year-old boy came to the playground to watch another boy fly a model airplane.[22] There were many old telephone poles surrounding a parking lot near the basketball court. The boy tried to

---

21. Orsini v. Guilderland Central School Dist. No. 2, Albany County, 360 N.Y.S.2d 288 (N.Y. App. Div. 1974).
22. Conway v. Saint Gregory's Parochial School, 235 N.E.2d 217 (N.Y. 1968).

climb a tree and when he let go of a branch and fell, a telephone pole fell on him and injured him. He sued the district for failing to provide supervision on the playground.

A custodian testified at the trial that the school principal had issued a warning on the last day of school to all students to avoid coming on the playground after school was out. In view of this testimony the New York court ruled that the boy was a licensee (one whose presence on the premises of another is permitted but not invited) and as such the school did not have the responsibility of furnishing supervision to him. It held, instead, the plaintiff guilty of contributory negligence.

The New York Supreme Court considered a charge against the school district of negligent conduct, for failure to provide supervision on a playground during the summer.[23] The plaintiff was a seven-year-old boy who was injured when three boys threw glass bottles at him that broke and cut his eyes. The school readily admitted that it did not provide either organized play or supervision during the summer vacation period on the playground.

The court upheld the school district by ruling that the proximate cause of the injury was the intervening act of third parties which was unforeseeable to the school. It dismissed the case in favor of the school district.

One of the few exceptions decided in favor of the plaintiff regarding playgrounds continues to be consistent

---

23. Crossen v. Board of Educ. of City of New York, 359 N.Y.S.2d 316 (N.Y. App. Div. 1974).

with earlier decisions that the school must provide safe playgrounds if not supervised ones.

William Cioffi was injured on the playground by an iceball thrown by another student.[24] The New York Supreme Court, Appellate Division, held that the school should have known that it needed to provide supervision under the conditions that existed.

One of the judges strongly disagreed because he felt that the school district did not have an obligation to provide supervision under the conditions. He argued that the boy could have entered the building instead of going on the playground where he knew a snowball fight was probable. When the area was used for recreational purposes the school supervised it, he argued, but the school could not foresee the injury that occurred. He concluded that snowballing is natural and not undesirable and only, if after notice of it, could, or should the school be held liable for failing to provide supervision.

The decision stood, however, and is in keeping with the past decisions of the courts regarding hazardous conditions on the playground.

Instruction

A. Inadequate Instruction

Stephen Fosselman sued his physical education teacher, the superintendent of schools, the principal, the school board members and the school district for injuries he suffered during a game of "bombardment."[25]

------

24. Cioffi v. Board of Educ. of City of New York, 278 N.Y.S.2d 249 (N.Y. App. Div. 1967).
25. Fosselman v. Waterloo Community School Dist. in County of Black Hawk, 229 N.W.2d 280 (Iowa 1975).

Stephen was a ninth grade student in Iowa and his class of 45 boys was separated into two teams to play "bombardment." The instructor placed four deflated volleyballs in the center of the court and lined each team up at the opposite ends of the gymnasium. According to the rules of the popular game, players hit by the balls were required to leave the game. The object of the game was to determine who was the last player to remain at the end of the game.

The plaintiff ran to the center court to get a ball and struck the knee of another boy. At the time Stephen was injured, the teacher was either at the side of the court or participating in the game. He did not see the injury take place but learned of it after several students found the injured boy in a dazed condition in the locker room. The plaintiff had "four fractures of facial bones, a depressed sinus and bruises to the left eye and surrounding area."

The boy and his father claimed that the defendants permitted a dangerous game to be played and required the plaintiff to play. Stephen admitted that he had played the game prior to his injury and agreed that his teacher had explained the game and its rules at the beginning of the year.

The Supreme Court of Iowa found no evidence that the instruction was inadequate or that more than one instructor was needed for the activity. It concluded that the defendants were not guilty of negligence and, therefore, dismissed the case against them.

Barbara Kobylanski was injured while attempting an exercise known as a "knee hang" on steel rings which were fastened to the ceiling.[26] She fell and injured her

---

26. Kobylanski v. Chicago Bd. of Educ., 347 N.E.2d 705 (Ill. 1976).

spine and subsequently accused her teacher of negligence
for failing to provide her with adequate instruction.

The defendant teacher and school district referred to
an Illinois Statute of the School Code in denying any
negligence. The statute specifically stated that:

> Teachers and other certified educational em-
> ployees shall maintain discipline in the schools.
> In all matters relating to discipline in and
> conduct of the schools and the school children,
> they shall stand in the relation of parents and
> guardians to the pupils. This relationship shall
> extend to all activities connected with the
> school program and may be exercised at any
> time for the safety and supervision of the pu-
> pils in the absence of their parents or guard-
> ians.

The Illinois Statute required "a plaintiff to prove
willful and wanton misconduct in order to recover damages."

The Illinois court ignored the plaintiff's argument
that "parental immunity" is eroding and not applicable
in the instant case. It interpreted the statute as applying
to the present situation since the teacher was directing
activities that were part of the school's program. It
therefore ruled that the plaintiff failed to prove that the
defendant's conduct was "willful and wanton." It also
found that the school district's purchase of liability
insurance did not waive immunity by declaring that:

> the existence or nonexistence of insurance is
> not a proper factor in determining liability.

Kevin Banks was an eighth-grade student in Louis-
ana where he was injured in the gymnasium before class

began.[27] Kevin came to class and joined several other students in diving from a springboard over folding chairs placed on top of each other. The boy hit the chairs and landed on his head instead of his feet and injured his spine.

At the time the plaintiff was injured, his teacher was preparing for the upcoming class by collecting valuables from students who were preparing to dress for class. He did not see the accident but when informed of it sent the boy to the principal who in turn, sent the boy home. He was hospitalized for ten days.

Evidence furnished during the trial proved the teacher was qualified and that the activity was approved for the class. The teacher had instructed the students adequately before the accident took place. Students were prohibited from participating in the tumbling exercise until they were properly dressed and the roll was called. Since the teacher had properly instructed all the students, including the plaintiff, the court surmised that the students were ignoring established rules of policy by attempting stunts without the teacher's permission.

The Louisiana court commented that:

> There is just no way that a teacher can give personal attention to every student all of the time.

It cited another Louisiana case in which the court favored a teacher although she had left her class unsupervised and an accident occurred. The court stated:

> The fact that every student is not personally supervised every moment of each school day

---

27. Banks v. Terrebonne Parish School Bd., 339 So. 2d 1295 (La. App. 1976).

does not constitute fault on the part of the School Board or its employees.[28]

It also consulted *Nash v. Rapides Parish School Board* in which the court said:

> As is often the case, accidents such as this involving school children at play, happen so quickly that unless there was direct supervision of every child (which we recognize as being impossible), the accident can be said to be almost impossible to prevent.[29]

The Louisiana court remarked that the present case was well within the "scope of the statements" listed above and ruled emphatically that neither the instructor nor the school district were guilty of negligence. It ordered the case dismissed.

In high risk activities such as wrestling or gymnastics, the quality of instruction and especially the qualifications of the physical education teacher are important factors in litigation. Lowry Stehn, a fifteen-year-old student at a private school in Tennessee was seriously injured during a wrestling match in class.[30] Sometime during the bout, his opponent, who was thirteen pounds heavier, executed an "agura" hold and either during or after its completion, Stehn suffered a broken neck and a severed spinal cord.

The United States Court of Appeals, Sixth District sitting in Nashville, Tennessee considered "whether the

---

28. *Supra* note 18.
29. Nash v. Rapides Parish School Bd., 188 So. 2d 508 (La. App. 1966).
30. Stehn v. Bernarr McFadden Foundations, Inc., 434 F.2d 811 (6th Cir. 1970).

operator of a private school is liable for damages resulting from injury to a student proximately caused by its negligence in failing to provide proper instruction and supervision in connection with the activity of wrestling and in conducting that activity."

The court carefully weighed voluminous testimony and cited as precedent a principle stated in *Rodriquez v. Brunswick Corporation*[31] in which an injured student was awarded damages. The court in that case commented that:

> Negligence is the failure to exercise due care, and this means due care under the circumstances of the particular situation. A teacher's superiority in knowledge and experience imposes responsibility in his dealings with students in which become an inherent element in measuring his compliance with due care which is required of him. A teacher may not, either by express instruction, or by his own example or his permission to others, teach a student to act in a manner which is unnecessary in the process of instruction and dangerous to safety.[32]

The federal court in the *Stehn* case considered such questions as the number of instructors needed to teach an eighth grade class, how much preparation and years of experience an instructor in wrestling might need and how much difference in weight between students in wrestling would constitute negligent conduct. It commented that proof of a failure to any one of the above would not necessarily prove that the defendant was

31. Rodriguez v. Brunswick Corp., 364 F.2d 282 (3d Cir. 1966).
32. *Id.*

negligent. As an example it stated that an instructor did not owe a student the duty to pair him against an opponent who was the same size.

After much deliberation, the Court found that there was sufficient evidence to prove that the proximate cause of the boy's crippling injury was the lack of proper instruction and supervision. It, therefore, awarded the plaintiff $375,000 and an additional $10,000 for Lowry's mother.

Arthur Darrow sued the school district in New York for injuries he sustained during a physical education class.[33] Darrow was playing a game of line soccer in the gymnasium when he ran into a player on the opposing team. The teacher divided the class into two teams and gave each player a number that corresponded to one on the other team. The teacher would then call a number and the members of the team with such a number would run toward the ball and try to kick it through the opposing team.

The plaintiff claimed that the teacher failed to give the class adequate instructions or demonstrations and the lack of proper instruction led to his injury. He produced an expert who testified that a game of this type required reasonable care and instruction on the part of the teacher. He stated that the teacher in a game such as this should emphasize to the participants that they:

> Must play the ball as much as possible with their feet, without any bodily contact, that they should not charge the ball to the point of bringing about bodily contact and that there

---

33. Darrow v. West Genessee Central School Dist., 342 N.Y.S.2d 611 (N.Y. App. Div. 1973).

should be no pushing, shoving, or rushing into each other.

The New York Supreme Court evaluated the teacher's statement that he failed to instruct the boys as to what to do when players arrived at the ball at the same time. For this reason it reversed the lower court's decision to dismiss the complaint against the teacher and ordered a new trial instead. The case was finally settled out of court and the plaintiff received compensation for his personal injuries.

B. Rules and Regulations

Jack Tashjian, Jr. was a third grade student in New York who was hit by a bat swung by a fourth grade student during a playground softball game, despite the fact that the school board passed a rule that prohibited third graders from participating in softball during recess.[34] The boy was rushed to the hospital where x-rays disclosed no fractures. About one month later, the plaintiff "suffered an epileptic seizure which was followed by recurrent seizures" which required hospitalization. Medical authorities testified that the blow the boy received from the softball bat was the cause of the seizures.

The court awarded the plaintiff $37,100 in damages for his injuries, holding the school district liable for failing to enforce its regulations prohibiting the third grade students from playing softball during recess.

---

34. Tashjian v. North Colonie Central School Dist. No. 5, 375 N.Y.S.2d 467 (N.Y. App. Div. 1975).

C. Assigning Students Activities Beyond Their Ability

In New York in 1975 Stephen Yerdon and his father named the superintendent, principal, physical education teacher and school district as defendants in a lawsuit.[35] The boy was injured when he fell during an activity known as "Ride the Horse." The plaintiff tried to convince the jury that the game was inherently dangerous and one that should not have been included in the physical education program. They charged the teacher with negligent conduct for assigning such an activity to the members of the class.

Both parties furnished expert witnesses with one contending that the activity was dangerous while others argued that the game was not inherently dangerous and reasonable for students of the plaintiff's age. The New York Supreme Court, Appellate Division, affirmed the trial court's verdict favoring the teacher and other defendants.

A seventeen-year-old girl, at White Plains High School in New York, was hurt in a gymnastic exercise called "jumping the buck."[36] The girl claimed that she had weak wrists and that she expressed her concern to her teacher about attempting the exercise. She contended that her teacher ignored her apprehension and directed her to try to do the stunt anyhow. The girl reported that her weak wrist collapsed and she fell forward and sustained painful injuries.

---

35. Yerdon v. Baldwinsville Academy and Central School Dist., 374 N.Y.S.2d 877 (N.Y. App. Div. 1975).
36. Cherney v. Board of Educ. of City School Dist. of City of White Plains, 297 N.Y.S.2d 668 (N.Y. App. Div. 1969).

The defendant school board argued that the doctrine of *respondeat superior* did not apply in this case. The New York court did not agree and answered that the school district could be held liable for the acts of the teacher, even though the teacher had not been named as a defendant. The lower court favored the injured girl but the Supreme Court of Westchester County reversed its decision and ruled that the defendant school district was not guilty of negligence.

One case settled out of court is worthy of consideration since the issues involved in it are of importance. A senior at a high school was participating in a required physical education class in 1971.[37] By his own admission and that of the teacher and classmates, he was not well coordinated nor the athletic type. His teacher described him as cooperative and not the type of person who took the easy way out or tried to avoid physical activities.

The student did not want to try a difficult stunt described as a "modified backflip" by his instructor. The instructor directed the members of the class to attempt every stunt if they wanted to pass the course. Not only did the threat of failure create an unfavorable climate toward such activities as the "backflip" but several members of the class testified that the instructor often berated students who could not do the exercises well. He reportedly called them "sissy" and made other embarrassing remarks to them. With this as a background, it is apparent why the student attempted the stunt although he feared the consequences.

---

37. New Jersey case settled in 1975 with the agreement that the name of the defendants would not be discussed with the amount of award paid the plaintiff.

The student landed wrong and broke his neck. When he went to the hospital he was treated for his injury, but due to alleged negligent treatment, he suffered additional injury and became partially paralyzed.

The student, whose parents were deceased, faced spiraling medical bills with no means of paying for the costs. The student sued the physical education teacher for his failure to properly instruct him in the gymnastic exercises, and the medical staff at the hospital that caused him additional injury, for malpractice.

The plaintiff's attorneys secured the testimony of experts in physical education who supported the instructor. They referred to Samuel Fogel's book *Gymnastics Handbook* in which he discusses gymnastics training. Fogel writes about a skilled or above average student, not a poorly coordinated one like the plaintiff when he states:

> Impatient teachers move too fast. It is important for a team to progress — but do not expect miracles. It takes time and patience to develop a sound team. Make up progress sheets for each boy and check him as he attains his goals. Don't push a boy into a trick on the bars or rings. Instead make sure he is ready for it, both mentally and physically.[38]

It was obvious, stated the experts as a group, that the plaintiff was neither ready physically nor mentally for the "modified backflip." A key point was the use of spotters in the class the day the accident took place. The instructor admitted that the spotters he used did not

---

38. Samuel J. Fogel, Gymnastics Handbook, Parker Publishing Co., West Nyack, New York, 1971 at 12.

have particular training as spotters other than the fundamentals they received in class during their four years of physical education.

Once again the authorities in physical education stress the importance of spotters when they say:

> The spotters' responsibility is to supply any force, motion, or principle that the performer fails to provide. When the gymnast attempts a new or uncertain move, he must feel confident that his spotter will not only protect him from injury, but will guarantee him success.
> If the spotter is committed to his role, his performer will gain confidence and the risk of major injuries will be greatly reduced.[39]

Fogel insists that "spotting" is learned by *constant practice* just as gymnastics is learned.[40]

One of the spotters testified about his position as spotter that:

> I was acting as a spotter when the plaintiff was injured. This was the first time we had ever learned it or were instructed in it. I had been a spotter before but not for backflips. This was the first time I had been instructed in the backflips. I did not want to do the backflip myself but I did it. It was one of the requirements.

He added that:

> about 10 or 15 minutes were spent by the teacher telling us about it and demonstrating it.

---

39. Gordon Maddux, Men's Gymnastics, Goodyear Publishing Co., Inc., 1970 at 16.
40. Fogel, *supra* note 38 at 13.

He concluded by commenting that:

> We tried to catch him but couldn't prevent his fall. I was never a spotter before for backflips nor had I performed backflips before.

A gymnastic instructor read the testimony and indicated that it was apparent that the two spotters actually flipped the student rather than spotted for him. He agreed with another gymnastic teacher that the lack of training of the spotters contributed heavily to the injury to the plaintiff.

The attorneys for the instructor and school district and the defendant medical team agreed to settle the case out of court. The school district paid $75,000 in damages and the insurance company representing the medical doctors paid $300,000. In addition the medical bills of the injured plaintiff were waived.

Summary

One of the leading causes of a lawsuit is the absence of the teacher from the classroom or playground. In these instances, the courts determine whether the teacher's presence would have prevented the accident. Absence alone does not constitute negligence on the part of the teacher. If a teacher is not able to use discretion in leaving a class, it would require a teacher to call for outside help for even very short absences. This would impose on the teacher a standard of care akin to an insurer rather than the standard of a reasonable and prudent parent. The courts consider the time, place, age, type of students in the class, the reason for the teacher's absence and the length of absence, as well as the teacher's ability to foresee danger in leaving a class alone.

During emergencies teachers should send for assistance rather than leave a class unsupervised when dangerous conditions or equipment are present. While teachers are urged to avoid as many hazards as possible, the courts recognize that physical education encompasses risks and physical hazards. It realizes that the system cannot be made "child-proof." The courts also realize that a teacher who acts prudently will find that the courts are just as much a shield as they are a weapon against him if he is negligent. Teachers should not have the constant threat of economic loss hanging over them as they attempt to perform their duties.

The courts have ruled that administrators do not owe students supervision for off-campus injuries that are not a part of the school program. Administrators are expected however, to formulate rules and enforce them for the safe conduct of the school program.

States which waive or modify immunity receive the majority of cases involving school accidents. These districts are expected to be insurers of the students' safety in all too many situations.

School districts are frequently involved in litigation involving playground-related accidents. The courts consistently rule that schools are not expected to furnish supervision during off-school hours for non-school programs. The exception comes when hazards exist on the playground and threaten the safety of the participants. In such instances, the schools are expected to close the playgrounds until the danger is remedied.

The courts expect school authorities to employ qualified teachers for physical education activities. The courts generally rule that a teacher's superior knowledge and experience impose a responsibility to deal with students in a safe and careful manner. Teachers are expected to teach students in the proper technique of an activity. A teacher may not teach a student to act in a manner that is dangerous either by instruction or by example.

School authorities are responsible for the enforcement of adopted rules and regulations that are designed to protect the students.

In high risk activities such as gymnastics, teachers are cautioned to adequately instruct, prepare and warn the students of the inherent dangers of a particular activity. Teachers should consider the student's ability and physical condition in assigning activities. Safeguards such as spotters, mats, etc., are necessary in the conduct of high risk activities. Teachers should use sound judgment and discretion when they assign various activities to all students.

4. Teacher-Related Issues

*A pilot should be able to land an airplane as well in
dirty overalls as in a neat uniform, and a teacher
to explain the Pythagorean theorem as well
in a T-shirt as in a three-piece-suit — but
the public's reaction to an official,
and a student's reaction to his
teacher, is undoubtedly affected
by the image he projects.*[1]

Many cases that go to the courts involve teacher-related issues and charge a violation of federally protected rights. In these cases the courts concentrate on the question of constitutional rights rather than the particular details of the case.

Discrimination in employment, working conditions and hiring procedures are common sources for litigation. Other issues involve the right of the school to suspend teachers when the enrollment at the school drops. Teachers also question suspensions that occur because of their mode of dress or appearance and the refusal to participate in extracurricular activities and coaching. Issues also involve a conflict of interest, a lack of cooperation and the use of corporal punishment.

Discrimination

A. Employment

Daniel Gavrin, a tenured teacher in physical education, was told in 1976 that he would be dismissed in mid-term

---

1. Miller v. School Dist. No. 167, 495 F.2d 658 (7th Cir. 1974).

because of the financial crisis in New York.[2] Gavrin was informed that a female teacher with less seniority would replace him to teach classes in girls' physical education. He was told that his name would be placed on a preferential list so that he would be eligible for employment if an opening in boys' physical education developed.

Gavrin appealed the decision to release him to the Commissioner of Education of New York in an attempt to seek reinstatement and payment of back pay. He argued that the school did not license physical education teachers according to sex but did keep seniority lists by sex. He claimed that the hiring of female teachers with less experience than he had represented discrimination based on sex.

Gavrin referred to Title IX of the Federal Elementary and Secondary Act that prohibited such discrimination by stating that a recipient of federal aid shall not:
1. classify a job as being for males or females;
2. maintain or establish separate lines of progression, seniority lists, career ladders, or tenure systems based on sex.

The Commissioner of Education considered an earlier New York case in which a physical education teacher was denied a job because he was a male.[3] The Commissioner of Human Rights ruled that the school had violated the Human Rights Law by hiring female teachers for girls' physical education classes. The Human Rights Board supported the Human Rights Commissioner's decision and made an interesting comment when it declared that:

---

2. In the matter of Daniel Gavrin (Decision No. 9321 of N.Y. Commissioner of Education, 1976).
3. Stein v. Board of Educ. of City of New York, 47 A.D. 2d 964 (N.Y. 1974).

The argument was proposed that pupils had to be 'touched' and that this, therefore precluded the complainant from teaching in a class of girls. This is sheer nonsense. First of all, no 'touching' is necessary in the teaching of such classes, and secondly if 'touching' were involved the propriety of it would depend on where, why and how.[4]

The Board of Education concluded in the *Stein* case that a person could not be denied a position to teach physical education because of sex "in relation to employment in a locker room or toilet facility used only by members of one sex."[5]

In Gavrin's case the Commissioner of Education noted that the school board did not issue certificates for teachers by sex and he found that physical education teachers were no exception to the policy. He stated that locker room duties cannot be used as a criteria for hiring. He then ordered the school to reemploy Daniel Gavrin. He also ruled that the seniority lists of male and female teachers be combined into one and directed the school to repay Gavrin the salary lost if the court found that a teacher with less seniority had been retained over him.[6]

B. Working Conditions

Jeanne Harrington taught physical education in Ohio for fifteen years.[7] She was informed that she was being transferred to another school to teach social studies. The

---

4. *Id.*
5. *Supra* note 3.
6. *Supra* note 2.
7. Harrington v. Vandalia-Butler Bd. of Educ., 418 F. Supp. 603 (S.D. Ohio 1976).

teacher had a hearing loss which she felt would hinder her in the new assignment and rather than accept it, she took voluntary disability retirement.

Harrington then instituted a lawsuit against the school for alleged discrimination in the facilities, salary, support for teachers and equipment the girls had available when compared to the boys. During the trial, testimony was produced that revealed that the girls' gymnasium was inferior to the boys' gymnasium in lighting and ventilation. The male instructors had private toilets and shower facilities while the plaintiff did not. In addition, the male instructors only taught physical education on a part-time basis while the plaintiff was a full-time instructor. The men, however, taught academic subjects in addition to their physical education classes.

The United States District Court of Ohio found that while the plaintiff had not proved discrimination in salary or job assignment she did establish that her past working conditions were definitely inferior to those of her male colleagues. It ruled that she was not due back pay or reinstatement to her former position because of her physical disability. However, it did award her $6,000 as compensation for the six years of discrimination in working conditions.

C. Hiring Procedures

Mary Shenefield applied for a teaching position in Wyoming but the principal hired a man who could teach physical education and coach. Shenefield submitted her case to the Wyoming Fair Employment Commission (hereafter referred to as Commission), and it agreed that discrimination based on sex had taken place. The District

Court of Sheridan County reversed the Commission's decision and the teacher appealed to the Supreme Court of Wyoming.

During the trial several factors that affected the school's decision were revealed. The principal testified that the plaintiff changed jobs frequently because she followed her husband wherever he took a new position. He described her as a "pushy, demanding type of person" who could not coach interscholastic activities or intramurals. In addition she would have required a substantially higher salary than the teacher they hired because of her degree and years of experience. The principal said that the teacher he hired had worked in the school system as a student teacher and was the type of person who could get along with the faculty. The school could hire him for $2,600 less per year than the plaintiff.

The Supreme Court of Wyoming referred to previous cases that considered similar litigation and upheld the principle that the courts will not interfere with the judgment of a school board in the employment or reemployment of a teacher "for any reason whatever or for no reason at all."[8] The Wyoming court then reasoned that a school board does not give up its freedom to choose the teacher it wants just because it advertises for a teacher. It then favored the school board's decision to hire the male teacher by indicating that:

> If it turns out that for reasons of economy, one applicant can fulfill the needs of the district at a

---

8. Shenefield v. Sheridan County School Dist. No. 1, 544 P.2d 870 (Wyo. 1976).

cost substantially less than another applicant,
even though the rejected applicant may on paper possess the greater qualifications, a selec-
tion of the less expensive teacher cannot be
said by any board or court to have been the result of discrimination on the basis of sex.

It then concluded that a school board has the discretion
of hiring a teacher who is able to perform additional
duties such as coaching in the school's program. A
school board must be able to select a teacher who is
personally attractive to it without the threat of discrimination leveled against it.

Suspension

A. Enrollment

Two Pennsylvania teachers were suspended because
there was a decrease in student enrollment at their
school.[9] The teachers appealed to the Commonwealth
Court of Pennsylvania arguing that a decrease from 724
students to 610 over a ten year period was not substantial
enough to justify their suspension.

The Pennsylvania court disagreed with them and
stated that a decrease of 114 students did warrant
suspension in areas where services were no longer needed.
The plaintiffs pointed out that, after releasing them, the
school hired two additional teachers to teach physical
education. The plaintiffs admitted that they had less
seniority than all but the newly hired physical education

---

9. Smith v. Board of School Directors of Harmony Area School
   Dist., 328 A.2d 883 (Pa. Commw. Ct. 1974).

teachers. No additional teachers were hired to replace them in their teaching, however.

The court commented that it is desirable for a school to realign an existing staff so that no one is released whenever possible. It did not know if this was attempted in the present case. The court did express dissatisfaction with the school district for rating only teachers with unsatisfactory records when the law required a rating of all teachers. It held, however, that the failure to rate all teachers did not change the suspensions in this instance. It then ruled that it would not interfere with the school board's discretionary action unless:

> the action is arbitrary, based on a misconception of the law . . . we find that the school board acted in accord with the law, with knowledge of the facts and did properly exercise its discretion.

B. Dress Code

Physical education teachers often question a school board's right to require a particular type of dress for its teachers. Many feel that the guarantee of the First Amendment to the United States Constitution protects their right to dress as they please.

Richard Brimley chose to teach his classes in casual clothes and gave his reasons for such a style of dress as a desire to:

1. Present himself to his students as a person not tied to 'establishment conformity';
2. Symbolically indicate to his students his association with what he believes to be the ideas of the generation to which the students belong, including the rejection of

many of the customs and values of social outlook of the older generation; and

3. Achieve a closer rapport with his students and thus enhance his ability to teach.[10]

After the teacher was reprimanded for violating an unwritten dress code, he submitted a grievance which his principal rejected. A written dress code was devised that included the following regulations for teachers to follow during the hours school is in session:

1. Dress should reflect the professional position of the employee;
2. It should be exemplary of the students with whom the professional employee works;
3. Clothing should be appropriate to the assignment of the employee, such as slacks and jersey for gym teachers.

Any teacher who felt that sportswear was appropriate for a particular teaching assignment was directed to discuss it with the principal.

A Federal District Court in Connecticut held the issue in the case to be whether the school board had the constitutional right to adopt a dress code and whether the First and Fourteenth Amendments protect the teachers' right to dress as they please. The plaintiff asserted that a teacher does have the right to dress in any manner his conscience dictates without interference from the state.

The Federal Court of Appeals for the Seventh Circuit Court, sitting in Chicago, Illinois, interpreted due process as it relates to a school dress code as an aspect of freedom

---

10. East Hartford Educ. Ass'n v. Board of Educ. of Town of East Hartford, 405 F. Supp. 94 (D. Conn. 1975).

on the part of the individual to select dress, hairstyle and general appearance. It also observed that a person's choice often reflects:

> a religious conviction, the expression of political faith, a national or family heritage, or simply a person interested in projecting a special image or character.[11]

The federal court in Illinois then made a timely observation regarding a school board's attitude regarding the appearance of its teachers by saying that if a teacher's style of dress has a detrimental effect on the educational process, the school board can put the teacher's interest behind that of the public interest. It then commented that students are compelled to attend school and therefore should not be forced to associate with people who are considered to be objectionable by their parents. Since the school board has the ultimate responsibility of protecting the students' interests it has the responsibility of making the decision as to the appearance of its teachers. It then stated that an employer could deny an employee public employment if the applicant's appearance is determined to be inappropriate for the job. This does not violate the due process clause, it concluded.[12]

The federal court in Connecticut referred to an opinion of Supreme Court Justice Black when he strongly declared that he doubted that the federal courts have the authority to interfere with the operation of the public school system. Black commented:

---

11. *Supra* note 1.
12. *Supra* note 1.

> Moreover, our Constitution has sought to distribute the powers of government in this Nation between the United States and the States. Surely the federal judiciary can perform no greater service to the Nation than to leave the States unhampered in the performance of purely local affairs.[13]

In the instant case, a United States District Court in Connecticut considered the opinions of the Illinois court and the United States Supreme Court regarding the issue of appearance involving Brimley.[14] It considered the fact that every local school board in every community has the authority and duty to provide the educational program for the children of that community. It then commented that parents expect teachers to set examples that children can follow and that teachers need to realize this in deciding on their dress. It noted that when school boards fail to adopt dress codes teachers often:

> arrive in the classroom wearing Bermuda shorts or similarly inappropriate forms of flamboyant dress.[15]

The federal court in Connecticut then explained that it realized that a teacher's success will not depend on whether he wears a coat and tie. The court compared it to a school board's requirement that teachers stand rather than sit while they are teaching. It declared that the school board had the right to enforce such a rule whether the public or teaching staff accepted it or not.

---

13. Carr v. Schmidt, 401 U.S. 1201 (5th Cir. 1971).
14. *Supra* note 10.
15. *Supra* note 10.

The court reasoned that teachers only work about six hours a day and remain free to dress as they choose the rest of the day. It then concluded with a strong statement that not only applied to the plaintiff, but to all teachers, when it vigorously declared that anyone who did not agree with the dress code regulation:

> is free to go elsewhere and find a school system where conformance to a dress code is not required.

It found the rule to be constitutional and not "overly vague or unenforceable" and that the due process clause had not been violated. It ruled in favor of the school board.

C. Appearance

Max Miller, a non-tenured teacher, claimed that the school board refused to renew his teaching contract because he wore a beard and sideburns.[16] Miller testified that the school board gave reasons other than his appearance for the action, but he argued that the real reason was his appearance. He contended that the Constitution of the United States protected his right to select his mode of dress and appearance. He pointed out that his style of dress and Vandyke beard were not intended as expressions of his race or ethnic background.

The United States Court of Appeals for the Seventh Circuit, sitting in Chicago, Illinois, stated that it did not know whether the teacher wore a three-piece suit or faded levis and "T" shirts since the only question that

---

16. *Supra* note 1.

concerned it was whether a federal judge had the power
to determine the issue. The court considered the issue to
be two-fold, as to whether:

1. an individual's interest in appearing as he
    pleases is an interest in liberty within the
    meanings of the Due Process Clause of the
    Fourteenth Amendment, and
2. a refusal or discontinuance of public em-
    ployment motivated by a disapproval of an
    individual's appearance is a deprivation of
    that interest.

The court noted that while an individual's desire to
select his particular style of dress represents "an interest
in liberty, it is nevertheless perfectly clear that every
restriction on that interest is not an unconstitutional
deprivation."

It commented that appearance from the earliest times
was restricted in some manner by laws, social pressures
and custom. It concluded that the limitations on restrictions of dress and appearance, the health or safety of the
public were a desire to:

avoid specific forms of antisocial conduct, and
an interest in protecting the beholder from un-
sightly displays.

It agreed with an individual's right to select his style
of appearance in a democratic society that encourages
diversity, but it reasoned that the same society can place
restrictions on that choice.

The federal court reasoned that while hairstyle may be
trivial and relatively unimportant to many people it
could be a factor in the hiring of an employee by the state
just as:

a pilot should be able to land an airplane as well in dirty overalls as in a neat uniform, and a teacher to explain the Pythagorean theorem as well in a T-shirt as in a three-piece-suit—but the public's reaction to an official, and a student's reaction to his teacher, is undoubtedly affected by the image he projects.

The court admitted that a school board might occasionally make mistakes when it devises rules on the dress style but it must have the freedom, nevertheless, to make this decision.

It then concluded that it would be foolish to think that federal courts could regulate the length of haircuts with more competence than the local officials in the fifty states.

The court upheld the regulations of the school board as valid and not a deprivation of any freedom.

D. Extra-Curricular Duties

Teachers frequently ask what the law requires when administrators add extra duties to their regular teaching assignments. Practices and policies vary with school systems regarding financial supplements as well as reduced work loads and other administrative procedures.

Gloria McCullough and Mary Drussell were offered teaching contracts with duties in extra-curricular activities added to the ones they already were supervising.[17] Both teachers objected to additional assignments and altered

---

17. McCullough v. Cashmere School Dist. 222 of Chelan County, 551 P.2d 1046 (Wash. App. 1976).

their contracts so that they were similar to the ones they had the previous year. The school district rejected the "altered" contracts and when the teachers refused to sign the original contracts within fifteen days, the district sought replacements for their positions.

The plaintiffs claimed that they were protected by a continuing contract law that guaranteed them "a preferential right in curricular positions, before considering new applicants for the same positions." The court ruled that the protection of a preferential right was too far removed from the teaching function to extend to extracurricular activities. It cautioned that the job offer regarding extra duties must be reasonable "so that the law does not become a sword or subterfuge in the hands of the district, defeating the intent of the legislature to create job security." It elaborated on this by pointing out that a teacher's preparation and experience must be considered before an assignment is made.

In this case, the Court of Appeals of Washington declared that the school district met the requirements of the preferential right when it offered to renew the plaintiffs' teaching contracts for girls' physical education. McCullough received a supplement to supervise a girls' activities program and to coach track. The school board added interscholastic track and basketball to her duties. Drussell received extra pay to coach girls' gymnastics, and coaching girls' basketball for grades 7, 8 and 9 was added to her new contract.

The court concluded that the plaintiffs were assigned reasonable contracts and their failure to accept them constituted an abandonment of their right of employment. It therefore supported the earlier decision of the superior court in favor of the school district.

E. Refusal to Coach

An interesting case took place in New Jersey when two teachers, Richard Dombal and Donald Doolittle, requested extra pay for coaching and, when the board refused, submitted their resignations from the coaching responsibilities.[18] The teachers complained that they were forced into involuntary servitude and sought help from the federal court. The court dismissed the case but recommended that the plaintiffs go to an advisory board for a hearing. The advisory board upheld the teachers' position but the board of education rejected the decision and a federal court, under a new complaint, upheld the school board. The court referred to a previous New Jersey case as to the basis for its decision. *In Re Rutherford Education Association*[19] the question of whether a teacher could refuse to work with extracurricular activities was decided in favor of the school district. The court ruled that extracurricular activities were part of the educational program of a school and one that was not negotiable.

In the present case, it was said that the decision in *Rutherford* was still valid and it did not give a teacher the right to refuse a coaching assignment. The duties must be accepted.

The Supreme Court of Utah in *Brown v. Board of Education of Morgan County School District* held in 1977 that a school district had the right to dismiss a teacher who resigned his position as coach when his contract called for both teaching and coaching duties.[20]

---

18. Nolpe Notes, Vol. 12, No. 6, June 1977.
19. In re Rutherford Educ. Ass'n, P.E.R.C., No. 77-17 (N.J. 1976).
20. Brown v. Board of Educ. of Morgan County School Dist., 560 P.2d 1129 (Utah 1977).

The court stated that the exception to the policy would be left to the school board, if for some reason it decided to divide the contract.

Since the school board refused to separate the teaching and coaching duties, the court upheld the board's decision to rule that the teacher had in effect resigned his contract to teach and coach.

F. Conflict of Interest

A school board passed a rule that a husband and wife, administrator-teacher combination represented a conflict of interest.[21] It therefore prohibited the two from working together in the same school. The board admitted that the principal was a "fair-minded" administrator but the fact that his wife taught physical education at the same school was not viewed as the best situation for the school or the morale of the faculty.

The court declared that the board had the right to provide a rule to prevent a conflict of interest. It ruled that the board's regulation was constitutional and upheld its policy.

G. Lack of Cooperation

A successful and popular coach became very unhappy when he was not named athletic director when this position became available.[22] From the time he was bypassed for the job, he reportedly refused to support the school administration. The defendant school board decided not to renew his contract, and the teacher-coach sued on the

---

21. Nolpe Notes, Vol. 10, No. 3, March, 1975.
22. Williams v. Day, 412 F. Supp. 336 (E.D. Ark. 1976).

basis of "constitutionally impermissible reasons." He charged that the board refused to rehire him because he protected students under his care from faculty mistreatment, that he objected to verbal abuse from spectators against an athlete (who was his son) and that his right of free speech was violated.

The defendants replied that an Arkansas law vested power in the school board to do whatever it considered best for the benefit of its students.

The United States District Court of Arkansas did not agree with the plaintiff's arguments and commented that he was unhappy and discontented because another man was given the position he wanted. It concluded that from the time he was denied the position, he showed a lack of control and failed to cooperate with the school officials and in general "created an intolerable situation for the athletic director, the principal, the superintendent, and the school board." The court reasoned that the plaintiff apparently decided that he would leave sooner or later but wanted the public to recognize the injustice that was put on him. As a result he was the center of turmoil. The board realized that he was a popular coach and tried to keep him until it felt that the situation had deteriorated.

The Federal court upheld the school board's decision not to renew his contract when it commented:

> It is a sad story. But it is the type of problem that confronts school boards, unfortunately, on not infrequent occasions—the type which usually involves the entire school community. This particular school community has finally resolved the problem. It cannot be said that it did so in an unfair or arbitrary manner. The matter should therefore remain at rest.

H. Corporal Punishment

The United States Supreme Court considered the question of corporal punishment and ruled in a highly controversial and emotional decision that teachers could administer corporal punishment to their students.[23] The highest court of the land held that corporal punishment did not come under the protection of the Eighth Amendment of the United States Constitution. It ruled that prisoners (*not students*) come under the guidelines of the Eighth Amendment that prohibits "cruel and unusual punishment."

The Supreme Court reasoned that school children may be required to attend school but they are free to leave during the day and at the end of the day. Children who are physically mistreated have the support of the other students and teachers "who may witness and protest any instances of mistreatment."

It elaborated on the issue by explaining that:

> In virtually every community where corporal punishment is permitted in the schools, these safeguards are reinforced by the legal constraints of the common law.

It concluded that in cases of excessive punishment:

> Public school teachers and administrators are privileged at common-law to inflict only such corporal punishment as is reasonably necessary for the proper education and discipline of the child; any punishment going beyond the privilege may result in both civil and criminal liability.

---

23. Ingraham v. Wright, 97 S. Ct. 1401 (5th Cir. 1977).

While the decision was vigorously opposed by several dissenting justices, it clearly established the legal parameters of corporal punishment which can serve as guidelines for all teachers.

An earlier case in Illinois reflects the courts' attitude toward excessive punishment.[24] A physical education teacher was found guilty of assault and battery charges upon a student. The boy's mother came to school to pick her son up and saw blood streaming from his nose and an eye swollen shut. He was taken to a hospital for treatment.

The Appellate Court of Illinois considered the evidence and found that while a teacher stands *in loco parentis* to his students, the teacher is held responsible to the same degree of reasonableness required of a parent who disciplines his child. It ruled that the physical education teacher exceeded the standard of reasonableness that was expected of teachers administering corporal punishment under Illinois law.

Summary

Teachers go to court frequently to resolve differences and physical education teachers are no exception as they seek judicial remedies for many issues. Teachers question alleged discrimination in employment procedures, working conditions and salaries. They often contend that their rights guaranteed by the United States Constitution have been violated by restrictions on the mode of dress,

---

24. People v. Smith, 335 N.E.2d 125 (Ill. App. 1975).

appearance, extracurricular duties and the use of corporal punishment in disciplinary action.

The courts consistently rule that a physical education teacher can teach either male or female students and efforts to hire a certain teacher by sex to teach students of the same sex represents discrimination. In like manner, seniority lists, career ladders and tenure systems must be free of sex bias.

Teachers are expected to have equitable salaries for similar work loads, working conditions, facilities and equipment. The courts do not favor superior conditions for one group over another. In some instances, damages were awarded to a teacher who the court judged to have worked under inferior conditions compared to those of other teachers in the school for several years.

The courts upheld the school board's right to release teachers in an area where they were not needed when student enrollment dropped significantly. While the courts recommend that the school board attempt to realign the personnel on hand, it leaves the decision to the school board. The exception comes when an action is judged to be arbitrary.

In litigation that involves dress codes and appearance, the interest of the public is placed ahead of a teacher's desire to wear a particular style of dress or hair length. The school must determine that the teacher's style is detrimental to the educational process. While the court admits that a school board may make occasional mistakes regarding appearance and dress codes, it reasons that the school board has the ultimate right to regulate such a policy. Dissatisfied teachers are urged by the courts to find a school system in which they are permitted to dress as they desire. The court does not believe it is more competent than the local school officials in matters relating to policy.

A school board is given the legal right to select teachers of its choice using various criteria such as salary and ability to perform certain duties. Teachers can be assigned extracurricular duties as long as the assignments are reasonable. A teacher's contract to teach and coach may be divided if the board agrees but if it does not, the teacher who prefers to do only one can be subject to dismissal. A school board can formulate a rule to prohibit a married couple from holding an administrator-teacher combination if it deems it to be detrimental to the best interest of the school.

Teachers may use corporal punishment to discipline students but it cannot be excessive. A teacher may still stand *in loco parentis* to the students, but the teacher must exhibit the same amount of reasonableness to a child as the parent who disciplines his child.

5. Administrative Issues

We will be forced to become marsupials, so that each of us will be able to carry in his pouch—a live and active lawyer in order to keep us out of trouble.[1]

Administrators and school board members face complex legal issues on a daily basis. A Federal District court in Pennsylvania commented on the recent flood of litigation against administrators when it said:

> Every act, every administrative decision of every state and local official is today threatened by federal litigation.[2]

Sanford Levinson, a lawyer who teaches at Princeton University, feels that people trust each other less today than ever before. He declares that "people used to trust school officials. Now they don't and they go to court."[3]

Administrators are sued for practically any and all reasons and this has caused Simon Rifkind, a former federal judge, to write that we may become so litigious a nation that eventually we will be forced to become:

> marsupials, so that each of us will be able to carry in his pouch — a live and active lawyer in order to keep us out of trouble.[4]

This chapter will consider issues related to physical education in which administrators and school boards have been named as defendants in lawsuits.

---

1. Star Ledger, Newark, New Jersey, July 3, 1977.
2. King-Smith v. Aaron, 317 F. Supp. 164 (W.D. Pa. 1970).
3. *Supra* note 1.
4. *Supra* note 1.

Student Refuses to Attend Class

Yvonne Ouinette attended all classes in Swanton, Vermont, except physical education, because she felt that a "student should have every right to do only what she wanted to do." [5] The principal tried to reason with her but she announced that she would not attend the class then or at any time in the future. Her father supported her and tried to persuade the school board to change required physical education to an elective program.

The school board listened to the girl and to her father's petition but emphasized that physical education was important and would remain a required subject in the first year of junior high school. The principal testified that he had notified Yvonne that she would be suspended from school if she chose to stay away from physical education class. The girl decided to accept suspension rather than participate in the program.

Several weeks later, the girl and her father took their case to court in an attempt to have her reinstated in school. The plaintiffs gave three reasons for her unwillingness to attend class. These reasons had not been discussed before and were:

1. Yvonne reportedly experienced difficulty in changing from the class which instantly preceded physical education and in reaching the class which followed within the time allowed;
2. Yvonne resented the lack of individual shower rooms and the resulting loss of privacy;
3. Yvonne was disinterested in competitive athletics and her father felt that compulsory participation would be detrimental both emotionally and academically to his daughter.

The principal reported that five of Yvonne's classmates had been influenced by her action and, while they came to class, they would not take part in any activity. He testified that he had repeatedly given the plaintiffs the opportunity to present their case and that the action taken was in no way capricious or arbitrary.

A United States District Court in Vermont referred to *Wood v. Strickland* in which the United States Supreme Court said:

> The system of public education that has evolved in this Nation relies necessarily upon the discretion and judgment of school administrators and school boards.[6]

The federal court stated that due process had been met and since this had been done there remained no issue for it to decide. It then concluded that the requirements of the Fourteenth and Fifteenth Amendments had been met and therefore the court favored the defendant principal and school board. It made an interesting observation when it said:

> While there is a legal entitlement to a public education provided by the State, free from impairment of protected liberties, there is no right under the paramount law to receive a public education on special terms and conditions designed by the student.[7]

Student Sues to Remove Failing Grade from Record

"C.G." was a student in New Jersey who missed three classes in physical education. According to school policy,

5. Ouimette v. Babbie, 405 F. Supp. 525 (D. Vt. 1975).
6. Wood v. Strickland, 420 U.S. 308 (8th Cir. 1975).
7. *Supra* note 5.

the boy was unable to return to the class for the balance of the school year.[8] The boy took two physical education classes the following year to meet the course requirements for graduation. The boy graduated but sued to have any notice of his suspension from physical education removed from his record. The New Jersey Commissioner of Education decided that the student had graduated and for this reason he denied the student's petition.

Request for Modification of Physical Education Upheld

A tenth grade girl in New Jersey trained for six years in the hope that she could qualify for the United States World and Olympic Ice Skating Team.[9] For fifty weeks each year "D.L." trained a minimum of 35 hours a week in ballet and ice skating. When school was in session the girl skated each morning from 4:30 to 8:50 a.m.

The school allowed her to attend a study hall in place of physical education from September through December but required her to attend after that date. The program in physical education consisted of "calisthenics, rope climbing and other strenuous exertions, in addition to her ice skating regimen." The girl testified that she became ill from all the physical activity and her family doctor diagnosed her condition as exhaustion.

The West Orange Board of Education agreed that the girl should be permitted to substitute another activity

---

8. "C.G." and "L.G." v. Board of Educ. of Borough of New Providence, Union County (Decision of N.J. Commissioner of Education, June, 1975).
9. "J.L." on behalf of "D.L." v. Board of Educ. of Town of West Orange, Essex County (Decision of N.J. Commissioner of Education, June, 1975).

for physical education during her training but pointed to a statute that prohibited this exception. The statute exempted only servicemen who had completed basic training or athletes on game days of the interscholastic season.

The Commissioner of Education noted that the school was in no way responsible for her ambitious training schedule but he recognized that the values of her training were important and desirable. He encouraged the school board to consider the vocational opportunities that could result through international and national competition. He declared that education should provide flexible programs to develop the whole child.

The Board agreed and referred to a statute that gave sanction to flexible programs in which it said:

> Each board of education shall conduct as a part of the instruction in the public schools courses in health, safety, and physical education, which courses shall be adapted to the ages and capabilities of the pupils.

The Board reasoned that handicapped students are not compelled to attempt rigorous play or contact activities and this in essence illustrated the flexibility of the statute. It felt that it was not only free to provide flexibility but actually required to do so. It therefore suggested that "D.L."'s program be adjusted to recognize her strenuous training schedule by allowing her to engage in less strenuous activities such as archery and other leisure-type activities.

The Commissioner directed the Board's medical advisor to provide "D.L."'s physical education teacher with information relative to her physical condition so a satisfactory program could be devised. He then ruled that

"D.L." could continue in the modified program as long as she trains for her ice skating program. The petition was approved.

Discrimination Charged in Physical Education Grade

A case is pending that will become commonplace since the adoption of Title IX in the schools. Coeducational classes are required with few exceptions, and rules and programs that differentiate by sex will be carefully scrutinized and seldom allowed.

Sharon Pinkham failed a course in physical education because she received a score of 45 on a badminton test and a zero for not taking a required test in tennis.[10] Sharon reportedly scored 88 in class participation and this category was weighed twice in the grade. When the zero and 45 were averaged with the 88 and 78 in skills, her average fell below 60 with 70 being the passing grade.

At graduation Sharon was handed a blank paper because she failed physical education. Sharon's problem was compounded when the college that originally accepted her notified her that it would refuse to accept her unless she received her diploma.

Sharon's mother testified that her three sons graduated from the same high school without taking such tests in physical education. The boys were graded on class participation and attitude. The girl and her mother charged the school with permitting unlawful discrimination and asked the State Department of Education to

---

10. Nolpe Notes, National Organization of Legal Problems in Education, Vol. 9, No. 7, July, 1974.

eliminate dual grading systems based primarily on sex. The case is still in the courts.

School boards are frequently asked to waive course requirements in extenuating situations. Exceptions are always subject to scrutiny by some students, and teachers of physical education often resent exceptions in their area.

In New York, Rose O'Brien was given permission to miss physical education after she was operated on for a back condition.[11] She was told that she could substitute credits from other courses to make up the deficit in physical education. The girl met all her academic requirements but lacked the credits in physical education because she failed to attend classes in two courses. As a result she lacked one-quarter of a credit in physical education which was necessary for graduation.

The New York Commissioner of Education favored the student by ruling that:

> It is well established that a student may not be denied a high school diploma solely on the basis of failure to complete four years of physical education where a valid reason for the deficiency is demonstrated.

Failing Grade Alleged to Cut-off Jeans

Joyce Scally failed a course in physical education and her father petitioned the Commissioner of Education to review the grading scale of the teacher.[12] According to a

---

11. *Id.*
12. In the matter of John Scally (Decision No. 9376 of N.Y. Commissioner of Education, 1976).

statement submitted by the teacher, he determined a grade on the basis of effort and motivation. He admitted that his grading system was subjective and difficult to evaluate objectively.

The girl's father alleged that his daughter failed the course because she wore short cutoff jeans. He added that his daughter had been denied due process and requested the Commissioner to permit his daughter and all students to wear whatever they chose.

The teacher answered the charge by saying that the girl would not have passed the course no matter what she wore to class. He agreed that her jeans were in poor condition and "potentially harmful to her and other students." Students in the class reported that the teacher would not allow students to wear cutoff jeans in any condition.

The Commissioner of Education of New York decided that the girl's grade was improperly calculated since points were taken off for her clothing. He directed the Board to review the physical education teacher's method of grading since the Board is the final authority on grades.

Locker Room Assault

School boards are being asked to provide safe facilities, equipment, proper supervision and qualified instruction. A recent case points to the vulnerability of school boards.

A member of a womans' volleyball team at Catholic University Law School in Washington, D.C. came to practice early and went to the locker room to dress for an intramural game. She saw a man in the locker room and asked him to leave. "He grabbed her, choked her and raped her."[13]

The woman, 24, went to court against the university alleging that the assault was caused by the failure of the school to furnish adequate security in the gymnasium. The jury upheld the woman's charge and awarded her $20,000 in damages. The university's attorney exclaimed that it was "a very bad precedent" and declared:

> A university cannot be the insurer of everyone who comes onto the campus.

He continued by commenting:

> I can't believe the law says you have to provide a bodyguard for every female student.

The university's president stated that the security budget was up 500 percent since 1970, up to $350,000 and while he did not want the campus to be in a "state of seige," he lamented the fact that:

> the courts are holding universities responsible for an amount of security higher than that demanded in the public domain.

Field Trips and Excursions

Students of every age participate in educational field trips and excursions. Off-campus activities, by their very nature, present some element of danger to the students and cause frustration among school people who question their legal status.

---

13. "The Price of Rape," *Time*, Sept. 6, 1976 at 32.

A high school graduate in California died during an ROTC summer camp conducted by the local school board.[14] The boy's parents insisted that the school was negligent for failing to provide adequate supervision. They claimed that supervision should be similar for activities on campus or off-campus. The school board did not agree with the plaintiffs and referred to a California statute that it felt gave them immunity for situations that occurred off-campus. The statute provided that:

> All persons making the field trip or excursion shall be deemed to have waived all claims against the district or state of California for injury, accident, illness, or death occurring during or by reason of the field trip or excursion. All adults taking out-of-state field trips or excursions shall sign a statement waiving such claims.

The California court defined a field trip as "a visit made by students and usually a teacher for purposes of first hand observation (as to a factory, farm, clinic, museum)." It compared this to an excursion which it defined as:

> a journey chiefly for recreation, a usual brief pleasure trip, departure from a direct or proper cause, or deviation from a definite path.

The court agreed that the 1972 Education Code protected a school district from liability but listed three exceptions:

1. when transportation is furnished to and from school or to sponsor a school activity off school premises;

---

14. Castro v. Los Angeles Bd. of Educ., 126 Cal. Rptr. 537 (Cal. App. 1976).

   2. responsibility or liability has been otherwise
       specifically assumed;
   3. the liability in the event of a specific under-
       taking is imposed only while such pupil is or
       should be under the immediate and direct
       supervision of an employee of such district.

The court recognized that it is impossible to provide
all the educational programs in today's schools entirely
on the school grounds. Students have the need occasionally
to share experiences away from school property. As a
result, the court noted, the school should provide protection and safety for the students under its care. However,
the court concluded that field trips or excursions on
which attendance is not required put students on their
own. If a school sponsors an activity and requires
attendance and gives credit for the activity, the district
assumes the responsibility for the safety of its students.

The California court considered all aspects of the case
and reversed the superior court's earlier decision which
favored the school district. It ruled that the parents of
the deceased should have the opportunity to prove that
the ROTC program was similar to the school band and
orchestra's program and therefore needed adequate supervision.

In New York, two college students drowned during an
unexpected storm in an extracurricular activity sanctioned
by the State University at New Paltz.[15] Representatives
of the deceased students sued the university for allegedly
failing to provide proper supervision and safe conditions.

----

15. Mintz v. State of New York, 362 N.Y.S.2d 619 (N.Y. App. Div.
     1975).

The two boys were participating in an overnight outing sponsored by the Intercollegiate Outing Club of America of which the New Paltz Outing Club was a part. For over ten years the outings had been held at Lake George without a fatality. The club had taken the usual precautions such as including a "motorboat escort and a flashing beacon light on a nearby island which served as a navigational aid." In addition, veteran canoers who had canoes furnished with lights were present.

The proximate cause of the unfortunate and tragic accident was the sudden squall that unexpectedly developed without warning on the lake. The New York court ruled that this unforeseen storm was the reason for the accident and subsequent death of the two students rather than negligence on the part of the State University.

Summary

Administrators and school boards face difficult decisions on an almost daily basis. Today, more and more issues are resolved in the courts. In general, the courts rely on the discretion and judgment of school authorities to formulate and implement educational policy.

When students refuse to participate in physical education the courts find that while the student has the right to a public education, there is no accompanying right to receive an education on special terms and conditions designed by a student.

In a dispute over the method of determining a grade, the court ruled that the school board was the final authority on grades and ordered it to review the teacher's grading procedure.

Schools were held responsible for supervision in its building and facilities, and to insure safe conditions for its students.

Field trips were distinguished as a visit by students for first hand observation while excursions were generally a pleasure trip for recreation. The court concluded that the school district is not responsible for students on field trips or excursions in which attendance is not required. The district does assume responsibility for the students' safety, however, if it requires attendance and gives credit for the activity.

6. Equipment and Facilities

*We cannot insulate our children from all risks
they may or may not encounter.*[1]

Students of all ages spend countless hours in gymnasiums and on playgrounds. Today more new facilities and equipment are available to students in physical education than ever before. When the equipment is properly used and maintained, it is an asset to all who use it. If the equipment becomes defective, however, it can lead to lawsuits when students are injured, and unsafe facilities also are common cause for litigation.

George Peters, in *Sports Safety II*, writes that the public demands a higher standard of care today than ever before, and what was once reasonable may now be considered negligence.[2] Peters cautions people who provide equipment and facilities for recreational activities that the "legal obligations vary from state to state, the attitudes of jurors vary from locality to locality, and the facts of each case are always different."[3]

As a possible solution when standards for equipment and facilities are considered, Peters concludes:

> Thus, clear statements as to what the specific
> law is . . . . can only mislead. Instead what is
> desirable is a general understanding of the

---

1. Partin v. Vernon Parish School Bd., 343 So. 2d 417 (La. App. 1977).
2. Peters, Liability in Informal Sports and Recreational Programs, Proceedings of the Second National Conference on Sports Safety, Chicago, Illinois, 1976.
3. *Id.* at 117.

relevant legal obligations and trends in the law.[4]

Various legislation has been enacted in different states in an attempt to deal with the problem of equipment and facilities. In this chapter some of the exceptions to the rule of governmental immunity will be considered in addition to the many duties the school owes to its various publics.

Dangerous or Defective Condition of Equipment

A. Cases Involving Equipment

Raymond Murray borrowed a bamboo pole from his physical education teacher so he could practice high jumping on the weekend when school was not in session.[5] Anita Bush and Raymond's sister returned to the school playground to ride bicycles. Anita watched Raymond jump and when his sister laughed when he missed a jump he became very angry. He threw the bamboo pole at his sister but hit Anita instead. The injured girl sued the physical education teacher because he failed to supervise the area after school when a dangerous piece of equipment was used.

The Court of Appeals of Indiana could not find that the bamboo pole was dangerous at all. It reasoned that if the pole was dangerous, so was a "book, a board, or a bamboo fishing pole." If her argument was valid, each piece of such equipment would need constant supervision. It dismissed the case against the physical education teacher and the Board of School Commissioners.

---

4. *Supra* note 2.
5. Bush v. Smith, 289 N.E.2d 800 (Ind. App. 1972).

William Siau, a tenth grade student in Louisiana impaled himself during a physical education class when he ran into a javelin left near a pathway on the football field.[6] A fellow student had finished working out with the javelin and left it in the ground out of the pathway of the field. He then went to the track to run a required 50 yard dash so he could participate in a softball game.

The plaintiff had not dressed for physical education and was told he could not participate in the activity of the class that period. The boy disregarded the teacher's directive and started to run on the field toward the student who was running on the track. One of the instructors saw him running and told him to stop. The plaintiff replied "that he could run anyway."

The plaintiff did not have his glasses on while he was running and as he approached the javelin he turned to look at the runners on the track. He ran into the javelin and received injuries.

The Court of Appeals of Louisiana considered all the facts of the case and held the plaintiff guilty of negligence. It found that the boy's negligence was the proximate cause of the injury because he did not obey the instructions of his teacher and failed to look ahead. The court defined negligence as:

> a failure to observe or do something that one ought to have observed and done, and would have done or noticed with ordinary care. . . . Although plaintiff was not required to keep his eyes glued on the pathway, he was required to look sufficiently well to see if his path was clear.

6. Siau v. Rapides Parish School Bd., 264 So. 2d 372 (La. App. 1972).

Since Siau's negligent conduct caused the accident, the court upheld the judgment of the trial court in favor of the defendant.

B. Public Building Exception

Two Michigan cases illustrate a question regarding governmental immunity and a "public building exception" statute. In Michigan, the statute provides that a governmental unit, such as a school district, can be liable for "bodily injury and property damage resulting from a dangerous or defective condition of a public building."

When Nancy Cody fell from a mini-trampoline and broke her arms, she sued the physical education teacher and the school district for forcing her to participate against her will, and the principal for delaying medical treatment.[7] The plaintiff referred to the "public building exception" and the school district answered the claim by stating that it was pursuing a governmental function and was thereby not liable for the injury. Michigan courts have held that school districts enjoy immunity from their negligent acts unless protected by statute otherwise.

The district answered the allegation that the defective condition of the building contributed to the plaintiff's injuries by replying that the mini-trampoline was merely an object in a building and did not qualify as an exception.

The court then answered a final contention that the school district purchased liability insurance and as a

---

7. Cody v. Southfield-Lathrup School Dist., 181 N.W.2d 81 (Mich. App. 1970).

result waived its immunity. The plaintiff charged that the purchase of liability insurance should constitute such a waiver or "governmental agencies are wasting a great deal of money protecting against risks that do not exist."

The Court of Appeals of Michigan answered this argument by saying that a school district needed such insurance as a protection against the "areas where the legislature had eliminated their immunity. . . . injuries resulting from motor vehicles accidents and defective buildings."

It responded to all the charges of the plaintiff by ruling that the doctrine of governmental immunity was valid and the equipment did not come under the "public building exception."

In 1976 another case came to court in Michigan regarding the "public building exception" when a boy was struck in the eye by an errant ball.[8]

The plaintiff, David Zawadzki, was playing tennis on a court in the gymnasium when a fellow student on an adjacent court inadvertently hit a ball at him. The gymnasium had two tennis courts lined off. The plaintiff contended that the school was deficient for not providing nets to separate the courts or some other safety device. The question became whether the school district breached a duty owed the student by the absence of a safety device and if this absence could constitute a "dangerous or defective condition."

A statute was added to encourage the repair of some defect that might exist in public buildings. It also set a

---

8. Zawadski v. Taylor, 246 N.W.2d 161 (Mich. App. 1976).

time limit of 90 days for the repair after the defective condition became known to the school authorities.

In this case, as in *Cody*, the Michigan court once again supported the immunity doctrine by ruling that the injury was caused by the activity in the building and not a defect in the building itself.

It stated:

> To hold otherwise would expand the 'building' exception into an operation or activities exception.

C. Failure to Repair Defective Equipment

The failure of a school principal to respond to a notice that a slide was defective on the playground and not having it repaired resulted in liability against the school board in the District of Columbia.[9] Tyrone Washington, a one and one-half-year-old child, was injured on the school playground on a sliding board. A piece of rusted tin that stuck out from under the sliding board cut the boy's finger and necessitated the amputation of the infant's finger.

A teacher at the school told the boy's aunt that she had informed the principal that the slide was defective several days before the accident. The defendants disagreed that the piece of tin raised from under the slide caused the injury. Instead, they argued that the separation of over a foot in length caused by the absence of two bolts caused the accident to the plaintiff. They also claimed that the teacher's statement to the boy's aunt constituted hearsay evidence and should be disregarded.

---

9. District of Columbia v. Washington, 332 A.2d 347 (D.C. 1975).

The District of Columbia Court of Appeals held that the testimony of the boy's aunt, reporting the teacher's statement, was admissible evidence. It found the school district guilty of negligence for failing to repair the slide within a designated time.

D. Statute Requires Notification of Injury

An interesting case in Iowa involved a weight machine in which a portion of the machine "disengaged from the rest of the device and struck a fourteen-year-old student in the mouth." [10] The boy lost two of his front teeth as a result of the accident. At the time of the accident, the physical education teacher was in the room.

The boy sued the manufacturer of the weight machine for $25,000 and the school district for $5,000.

The plaintiff failed to meet the requirements of a statute stating that "a claim for a tort action for injury or death must begin within three months of the injury unless there is a written notice to the governing body within 60 days after the death or injury stating the time, place and circumstances."

The plaintiffs argued that the teacher reported the details of the accident the day it happened to the assistant principal and that the boy's mother notified the superintendent the following day. They argued that the failure of this notification to meet the statutory requirements constituted a violation of the plaintiff's due process and equal protection.

The Iowa court explained the reason for the strict adherence to the time limit of the statute by stating that:

---

10. Shearer v. Perry Community School Dist., 236 N.W.2d 688 (Iowa 1975).

> such notice requirements protect the public treasury from stale claims, permit prompt settlement of meritorious claims, avoid unnecessary litigation, facilitate planning of municipal budgets, and ensure that notice reaches the public officers with responsibility to deal with them, enabling such officers to remedy defects in municipal property before other persons are injured.

The justices, although divided in their opinion, finally ruled in favor of the school district. Several justices disagreed with the court's rationale and pointed out that:

> From time immemorial the status of a minor of tender years has been recognized in law to be different from that of one of more mature years. The law recognizes that up to the age of seven years a child is incapable of such conduct as will constitute contributory negligence, and our courts have uniformly so stated the law in their instructions to juries.

They also stated that:

> The minor is accorded special consideration in the field of torts.

The Supreme Court of Iowa then quoted from *Rosenau v. City of Esterville,* in which the court commented:

> In these two cases where the two principles collide—where statute and child meet—the better reasoned decisions hold a child is not to be charged with negligence per se even though his conduct may involve violation of a statute which relating to an adult would require application of that rule.[11]

---

11. Rosenau v. City of Estherville, 199 N.W.2d 125 (Iowa 1972).

The majority of the justices in the instant case, however, ruled that the school officials' knowledge of the injuries to the plaintiff did not constitute compliance to the statute requiring written notice. It found that the legislature could put adults and minors on equal basis with regard to the statutes of limitations. It therefore favored the school district.

Unsafe Facilities

It would be impossible to describe all the situations that cause facilities to be unsafe. The teacher, administrator and school district must therefore, be on guard to make themselves aware of potential hazards.

A. Duty of School to Licensee

A young boy attempted to lift a ladder on the playground that weighed over 250 pounds.[12] A corporation had been contracted to install the horizontal ladder on the school playground and after digging the holes, had at the end of the workday, left it on its side on the playground. The school principal notified the students that they were not to come on the playground until after the equipment was put in final form.

An eight-year-old boy came on the playground the following day, which was a non-working holiday, and attempted to raise the ladder. The ladder fell and the boy and several others were hurt.

The New York court found the school district not guilty and ruled also that the company employed to install the equipment was likewise innocent of the charges against it. The court ruled that the infant plaintiff:

was a licensee on the school property and that
the defendant company owed the infant
plaintiff no greater duty than to avoid the
maintenance of traps, hidden dangers, or
wanton or reckless conduct, and that the horizontal ladder while lying on the ground, was
not an inherently dangerous article.

B. Duty of School to Invitee

Occasionally situations come before the courts that
involve a person who is classified as an invitee (one who
is at a place at the invitation of another).

Debra Cappel, a five-year-old girl and several other
children attempted to lift a field hockey cage on the
playing field of a junior high school in New York.[13] The
field hockey cage was not anchored or secured to the
ground and it fell on the girl and injured her. The
plaintiff once before had tipped over the cage which was
approximately "seven feet tall and twelve feet high,
constructed of heavy galvanized steel pipe."

The court favored the plaintiff because, unlike the
instance of *Goldstein*,[14] an earlier case in which the
principal involved had warned the students to stay
away, the school in the instant case actually invited
students to use the field when school was not in session.
In this case the apparatus could be lifted by children
while the one in *Goldstein* weighed over 250 pounds and
was practically impossible for young children to lift.

---

12. Goldstein v. Board of Educ. of Union Free School Dist. No.
    23, Town of Hempstead, 278 N.Y.S.2d 224 (N.Y. 1966).
13. Cappel v. Board of Educ. of Union Free School Dist. No. 4,
    Northport, 337 N.Y.S.2d 836 (N.Y. App. Div. 1972).

In the *Cappel* case, the Appellate Division reversed the lower court's decision, and granted the plaintiff a new trial. The court felt that the school owed the children a duty to provide safe premises since the school understood the "known propensities of children to climb about and play."

C. Duty of School to Teacher

Carol Shelton, a Louisiana school teacher, sued the school superintendent for injuries she received on the school parking lot which was used for physical education due to limited space.[15] The area was paved with asphalt but covered in some places with loose gravel. In addition there were many "potholes" on the parking lot. She contended in her lawsuit that the school failed to provide a safe and adequate facility for the students and teachers in physical education. She claimed that the members of the school board knew that the conditions were unsafe but did nothing to repair and correct the situation.

The defendant superintendent and school board requested the court to dismiss the case since they felt they did not owe the teacher a duty to provide a safe place for her to work.

The superintendent furnished a document that revealed that any repair or renovation was the responsibility of a Building and Grounds Committee. If the Committee approved any recommendation for repair, it then presented it to the board for the allocation of funds. If the

---

14. *Supra* note 12.
15. Shelton v. Planet Ins. Co., 280 So. 2d 380 (La. App. 1973).

recommendation was approved, the board put the work on a bid and then, according to established procedure, issued a contract. The board was the only agency that could make the decision to do the work.

The state of Louisiana has established the policy that:

> an executive officer of an employer owes no duty as such or individually to an employee to provide him with safe working conditons; his duty or obligation in that regard, are due exclusively to the employer.

The Court of Appeals of Louisiana held that no action could be taken against the defendants since:

> the school board had the sole authority to approve the repair and renovation of school board property and to provide funds thereto.

D. Duty of School to Protect Students on Premises

An elementary student in Oregon fell from a platform in the center of which there was a hole.[16] The platform was about six feet off the ground. The plaintiff, Leo Becker, admitted that he played on the platform although he knew that there was a playground rule against students "jumping across this opening in the platform."

The defendant stated that the boy knew the risks that existed and assumed them in addition to being guilty of contributory negligence.

The plaintiff testified that another student had been injured in the same manner and that the school should

---

16. Becker v. Beaverton School Dist. No. 48, 551 P.2d 498 (Ore. App. 1976).

have known the platform was dangerous. The principal reported that a student who had been known to feign illness and who was very dramatic about injuries that did not exist, reported it, but that this type of individual did not give the school what it had considered reliable testimony that the platform was dangerous.

The Court of Appeals of Oregon agreed with the defendant school district and favored it by affirming the lower court's decision dismissing the case.

In another Oregon case Robert Quigley sustained injuries when stall bars in the gymnasium fell upon him.[17] Evidence revealed during the trial that the stall bars were unfastened. The question at the trial was whether or not the stall bars presented a dangerous condition and if the teacher was aware of the fact that they were not fastened to the gymnasium walls.

The apparatus consisted of horizontal metal bars about nine feet high that were used in the physical education program of the school. The bars had been delivered the previous day but workers had not yet fastened them to the walls.

The plaintiff, a twelve-year-old boy, alleged that his teacher failed to furnish his physical education class with sufficient supervision. He pointed out that the teacher's knowledge of the dangerous condition of the apparatus and failure to exercise reasonable care to protect the members of his class constituted negligence.

The jury was given instructions regarding contributory negligence much to the opposition of the plaintiff. The plaintiff also objected to the testimony by the defendant that the gymnasium was safe prior to the injury.

---

17. Quigley v. School Dist. No. 4573, 446 P.2d 177 (Ore. 1968).

The Supreme Court of Oregon affirmed the circuit court's judgment in favor of the defendant.

E. Duty of School to Foresee Danger

Three 1977 cases give the most recent position of the courts in New York, Minnesota and Louisiana toward unsafe facilities and pupil injuries.

A tree fell on a Sunday on the property of Simpson Public School in Simpson, Louisiana.[18] On Monday, the school janitor arrived at the school at 7:00 a.m. and immediately removed all the tree but the stump, which was smooth and rounded at the top and a few branches and pine cones. The janitor testified that he did not report the tree stump as dangerous because he felt it was not a hazard to anyone.

When the teacher in charge of the supervision on the playground saw the stump she called the 90 students together and told them not to play around the stump. She testified that the stump did not concern her but the limbs and pine cones might cause one student to injure another. She stood about 30 feet from the stump during the entire recess period. When she saw the infant plaintiff near the stump she "scolded him for disobeying her." After a while the plaintiff showed his teacher a bruise on his stomach. The boy became ill later in the day and his teacher attributed it to a virus that was going around the school. He was operated on later that night for a "lacerated pancreas."

The court reiterated the principle that reasonable

---

18. *Supra* note 1.

supervision must be "commensurate with the age of the children and the attendant circumstances."

It stated that:

> There is no requirement that the supervisor, especially where the play of some ninety children is being monitored, have each child under constant and unremitting scrutiny.

The Court of Appeals of Louisiana found little merit in the plaintiff's charge that the school board allowed a hazardous condition to exist on the playground. It agreed with the trial court's conclusion that:

> A stump in itself is not of a hazardous or dangerous nature to warrant the concern which the plaintiff would have the court to believe. . . . In a rural area such as Simpson, trees are predominant. Trees and their components are everywhere. As such, children are going to play in and around them. In doing so, this doesn't cause parents much concern. We then, as parents, should not expect more of others than we do ourselves. We cannot insulate our children from all risks which they may or may not encounter.

The court of appeals affirmed the lower court's decision for the defendants by concluding:

> the school board cannot foresee and guard against all the dangers incident to the rashness of children. It is not the insurer of the lives or safety of children.

F. Duty of School to Inspect Facilities

Lavonne Kingsley sought to recover damages for injuries she sustained when she climbed up a locker to "retrieve her coat and her finger caught on the metal portion on top of the locker as she attempted to jump down from locker."[19] The District Court of Minnesota rendered a judgment in her favor and the school district appealed.

Lavonne's locker was located near the principal's office and evidence revealed that students kept books and clothes on top of the lockers although the school had a regulation against it. The prinicipal testified that he "patrolled the halls from time to time to enforce the regulations concerning objects on top of lockers and children going to the locker during class periods."

The plaintiff noticed that her coat was on top of her locker and she tried to retrieve it and tore the skin and tissue from her finger. All that remained of her finger was muscle and bone.

The school custodian testified that there was a piece of metal protruding from the top of the locker. Evidence was produced that substantiated the girl's claim that she tried to get the principal to find usable hangers for her coat and help prevent people from throwing her coat on top of the locker. The plaintiff, therefore, was absolved of any negligence.

The school district admitted that a school has a duty to inspect and maintain the equipment, building and grounds for the protection of the students. It argued, however, that the locker was not defective and that there was a lack of evidence that the locker caused the plaintiff's injury.

---

19. Kingsley v. Independent School Dist. No. 2, Hill City, 251 N.W.2d 634 (Minn. 1977).

A student was allowed to state at the trial that school officials attempted to improve school discipline after the accident. The school district objected on the ground that this statement abused discretion and required a new trial. The court referred to a rule stated in another Minnesota case that pointed out:

> where the case is being tried by a jury, trial courts must exercise great caution in admitting evidence of repairs made or precautions taken after an accident for the purpose of showing the feasibility of precautionary measures. However, the trial court is entitled to weigh the need for such evidence against that risk that the jury may improperly infer negligence therefrom. Hence, the trial court's ruling on such evidence will be upheld except upon a showing of abuse of discretion.[20]

The Supreme Court of Minnesota commented that the testimony of the student involved the issue of supervision and held that there was enough evidence to find that the school district failed to inspect and maintain the lockers. It therefore affirmed the judgment in favor of Lavonne Kingsley.

G. Duty of School to Issue Warnings of Danger

Kenneth Zaepfel, a nine-year-old boy, went sledding in December on the school grounds of a city high school in New York.[21] The children in the neighborhood had the

---

20. Faber v. Roelofs, 212 N.W.2d 856 (Minn. 1973).
21. Zaepfel v. City of Yonkers, 392 N.Y.S.2d 336 (N.Y. App. Div. 1977).

choice of two hills for sledding. Kenneth tried the first hill, which was popular with most of the children, and then moved to the other hill with two of his friends. The boy was aware that the school authorities had left a fence near the bottom of the hill. Although it was a snow fence, it had been placed there as a crowd control measure during the football season. It was customary to remove it after the final game on Thanksgiving Day, but for some unknown reason it had been left there.

Kenneth came down the hill and caught his leg on a "bent rusty pole which was embedded in the ground and supported a portion of the fence." He admitted during the trial that he did not see the fence.

The New York Supreme Court reasoned that the failure of the plaintiff to notice the fence can be attributed to "momentary forgetfulness" and not negligence. In addition, it felt that the trial court's decision to dismiss the charge of contributory negligence was in order. It ruled that a nine-year-old boy cannot be expected to exhibit the same standard of care and caution as an adult.

It therefore found the school district guilty of negligence for failing to remove the fence and for not posting signs warning students of the dangers that existed on the playground.

Accidents at Colleges

Brian Mortiboys attended St. Michael's College in Vermont on a full athletic grant for basketball.[22] The

---

22. Mortiboys v. Saint Michael's College, 478 F.2d 196 (2d Cir. 1973).

college was a liberal arts college for men located in Colchester, Vermont.

The college had two outdoor ice hockey rinks although it did not sponsor an intercollegiate hockey team. The students used the outdoor ice rinks for pleasure and occasionally played "pickup" ice hockey games among themselves. During the trial, testimony indicated that employees of the college flooded the rinks several times a week during very cold weather. The employees scraped snow off the rinks whenever necessary and checked them daily.

One afternoon in February, the plaintiff and another student walked over to the rink and looked for friends in the hope of playing an informal game. They found several others and skated for some time on the rough ice. The plaintiff was skating rapidly when he suddenly hit a small lump of ice, fell and injured himself seriously.

There was no testimony that anyone had seen the lump of ice but the court speculated that:

> Outdoor ice is exposed to the vicissitudes of the weather and the accumulations caused by skaters using the surface. It necessarily becomes rough during such use. It is a matter of speculation what caused the lump to be formed and whether it had been there for any substantial length of time.

The court commented on the claims made by the plaintiff that an indoor ice rink needs expensive equipment such as a "Zamboni" (a snow machine that scrapes the surface of the ice and costs over $10,000). It concluded that a small liberal arts college like St. Michael's could not be expected to supply such expensive equipment and it felt that the duty put on the college was reasonably adhered to in this case.

The court also pointed out that:

> In order to impose liability for injury to an invitee by reason of the dangerous condition of the premises, the condition must have been known to the owner or have existed for such a time that it was his duty to know it.

The court noted that the Vermont court has been:

> increasingly liberal in holding the owner of premises liable to business visitors. The defense of assumption of risk, especially, has been narrowed. But the duty owed to a business visitor or other invitee is still to keep the premises reasonably safe.

It ruled that there was no proof that the lump of ice had existed for a long period of time that would have required the college to discover or remedy it. It reversed the United States District Court's decision which favored the injured boy and ruled instead in favor of St. Michael's College.

Cumberland College in Kentucky appealed the Circuit Court of Kentucky's verdict in favor of a student injured in a physical education class.[23] The lower court had awarded the plaintiff $10,000 for the injuries the girl sustained when she fell as the result of a sticky substance on the gymnasium floor. During the trial, witnesses reported that a foreign substance the "size of the top of a tea cup" was found in several spots near where the girl

---

23. Cumberland College v. Gaines, 432 S.W.2d 650 (Ky. 1968).

fell. It was a sticky liquid and no one saw the spots before the accident took place.

The Court of Appeals of Kentucky considered numerous cases dealing with substances on the premises of various places such as clubs, restaurants, banks, etc. in which a plaintiff was an invitee as was the plaintiff in the instant case. The court declared:

> However, where it is not shown that the condition was created by the possessor or under his authority, or is one about which he has taken action, then it is necessary to introduce sufficient proof . . . . that the condition existed a sufficient length of time prior to the injury so that in the exercise of ordinary care, the possessor could have discovered it and either remedied it or given fair adequate warning of its existence to those who might be endangered by it.

It felt that this was not clearly demonstrated in this case and that the injured student did not prove negligence against the college just because she was injured in a fall.

It then reversed the lower court's decision to award the girl $10,000 by dismissing the case against Cumberland College.

A major snow storm covered Husson College in Bangor, Maine and the 42 inches of snow prompted the college to cancel classes.[24] The maintenance department of the college spent hours attempting to clear the snow from the walks and roads at and around the college.

Lawrence Isaacson went to the cafeteria from his dormitory room and saw that the walks had been cleared

---

24. Isaacson v. Husson College, 332 A.2d 757 (Me. 1975).

of snow except for some snow that the wind had blown back. On the way back to the dormitory, the plaintiff fell on a patch of ice which he claimed he did not see because of a lack of illumination on the walk.

The plaintiff was in extreme pain and was immobilized with a cast and later walked with crutches. In the spring he underwent knee surgery for a "torn lateral semilunar-cartilage in his right knee." He spent considerable time rehabilitating his knee, but was left with impairment of twenty-five to thirty percent of his knee. He testified that his knee continued to swell whenever he attempted to participate in sports.

The director of the college's physical plant reported that his crew did not sand the walkways and that the area where the plaintiff fell was "essentially dark."

The court referred to the law in Maine regarding the liability of a landowner. The law was as follows:

> A possessor of land is subject to liability for physical harm caused to his invitees by a condition on the land but only if he:
> (1) knows or by the exercise of reasonable care would discover the condition and should realize that it involves an unreasonable risk of harm to such invitees, and
> (2) should expect that they will not discover or realize the danger, or will fail to protect themselves against it, and
> (3) fails to exercise reasonable care to protect them against the danger.

After reviewing the decision of the superior court, the Supreme Court of Maine ruled that it agreed with the lower court and held that the award of $12,000 was not excessive and "grossly disproportionate to the plaintiff's medical expenses of $1,674.70." It denied the college's appeal.

Summary

The public is demanding a higher standard of care than ever before and what was once reasonable, may now be considered negligence and this puts added responsibility on schools to inspect and maintain equipment, buildings and facilities. More equipment is available today for participants of physical education than in previous years. Failure to correct or repair a defective condition can lead to liability.

The courts have ruled that children who use facilities and equipment cannot be insulated from all the risks which they may or may not encounter. The courts realize that school authorities cannot foresee and guard against all the possible dangers that can occur by the impulsiveness of children nor can schools be the insurers of the lives or safety of children.

When people use equipment or facilities as "licensees," the school owes that person no greater duty than to keep the facility free from hidden dangers or wanton or reckless conduct.

The school has the obligation to foresee the known propensities of children who use its facilities and equipment and is required to warn them of dangers that exist.

The dangerous condition of premises or equipment must be known to an owner to exist for a period of time in which it would be possible for school authorities to correct the problem.

7. Water-Related Accidents

*Drowning is not such an occurrence which in the
normal course of things happens only if
there is negligence.*[1]

Over 100 million Americans take part in some water-related activity each year. Participation in such sports as swimming, fishing, boating and scuba diving is at an all-time high. Public schools alone report operation of more than 25,000 swimming pools, and the number increases each year. In the course of these activities some 7,000 persons drown each year. Water-related accidents are second only to motor vehicle accidents in causing deaths among Americans aged 4 to 44.[2] For these reasons this chapter gives separate consideration to the accidents that occur in swimming pools and ponds, on outings in which water-activity is included and in water-skiing activities.

Swimming Pools

Peter Wong was enrolled in a summer swimming program sponsored by the local school district and the federal government.[3] His body was discovered in the deep end of the pool and an attempt to revive him failed. The boy's parents sued the school district for hiring lifeguards who they claimed were inattentive and incompetent.

---

1. Wong v. Waterloo Community School Dist., 232 N.W.2d 865 (Iowa 1975).
2. *Basic Rescue and Water Safety,* The American Red Cross, 1974.
3. *Supra* note 1.

The Iowa jury was instructed to determine whether the school district failed to provide competent and adequate supervision at the pool. The court reviewed the qualifications of the seven people assigned to supervise the seventeen students and found them to be adequate. The court made an interesting comment when it said:

> Drowning is not such an occurrence which in the normal course of things happens only if there is negligence.

It then listed several factors that contribute to swimming accidents, such as:

1. the inherent dangers of swimming;
2. the possibilities of bodily malfunction on the part of the victim;
3. the lack of control over the swimmers who might cause or contribute to the misadventure;
4. the victim's own negligence.

The Supreme Court of Iowa upheld the judgment of the lower court and found that the lifeguards were qualified and no evidence of negligence could be found. It favored the school district.

In Kentucky, Larry Durham was found at the bottom of the indoor swimming pool at Murray State College by a fellow student.[4] Several students helped the lifeguard get the boy's body out of the pool. During the frantic rush to remove him from the water, the group let his head strike the deck of the pool. When the boy was turned over in preparation for resuscitation, they noticed

---

4. Durham v. Commonwealth of Kentucky, 406 S.W.2d 858 (Ky. 1966).

blood streaming from his nose and ear. His death was reported to be caused by a blow on the head.

The parents of the deceased contended that their son was at the bottom of the pool because the lifeguard on duty failed to provide adequate supervision.

Evidence at the trial disclosed that the lifeguard was qualified by proper certification and years of experience. There was evidence that some panic did take place as the boy was hastily removed from the pool. The Kentucky court, after deliberation, ruled that there was not sufficient evidence to support a charge of negligence against the lifeguard or board of regents. It dismissed the case and favored the defendants.

Arlee Russell was enrolled in a required swimming class at Morehouse College in Georgia.[5] The physical education teacher assigned several members of his varsity swimming team to assist him in teaching the class of non-swimmers. Although the student assistants all were strong swimmers, none were properly certified by the American Red Cross for instructional duties.

On the day of the tragic accident, the instructor informed the class that two of the student assistants would handle the class. He then divided the class into two groups by ability. Those who had learned to swim were placed at the deep end while the nonswimmers were sent to the shallow end of the pool.

Although Arlee was a nonswimmer, he lined up with the swimmers at the deep end and jumped into the pool. He sank to the bottom and drowned. It was three to four minutes before a swimmer discovered his limp body at the bottom of the pool. His body was retrieved by one of

---

5. Morehouse College v. Russell 136 S.E.2d 179 (Ga. App. 1964).

the student assistants who immediately administered artificial respiration, but to no avail.

Arlee's mother insisted that the teacher and college were guilty of negligence for failing to properly supervise the pool. The defendants blamed Arlee for assuming the risk by attempting to swim in the deep end of the pool when he knew he "struggled to keep afloat."

The Court of Appeals of Georgia denied the defendants claim against Arlee because it reasoned that the defendants had a greater responsiblity to a student in a required class of physical education than to a "mere volunteer or trespasser." The court then answered the charge that the lifeguards failed to revive Arlee and were guilty of negligence. It noted that the student assistants were obligated to try to restore life in the stricken swimmer but insisted that they were not required "to be successful in such attempt."

The college claimed immunity from suit by virtue of the doctrine of charitable immunity. The court denied this defense and ruled that Arlee's mother could sue the college for the untimely death of her son up to the amount of liability insurance it had. The case was finally settled out of court and payment was made to the plaintiffs.

A summer school student at the University of Miami suffered a crippling injury when he severed his spinal cord when he landed on his back in an empty swimming pool.[6] The student had spent most of the day drinking

---

6. Boyce v. Pi Kappa Alpha Holding Corp., 476 F.2d 447 (5th Cir. 1973).

beer with fellow students. Later he went to a nearby
fraternity house that had a pool which was open to any
fraternity member who wanted to swim in it. When the
student jumped into the empty pool in apparent "horseplay" he did not know that the water had been drained so
the pool could be cleaned.

The plaintiff sued the fraternity for violating a city
ordinance that required a pool to be protected by a screen
or fence at least four feet in height. The ordinance also
required the gates to be locked when the pool was not in
use. The plaintiff claimed that the lighting around the
swimming pool was inadequate and that the fraternity
failed to warn people that the pool was empty and
therefore dangerous. He argued that this negligence
constituted "willful and wanton" conduct and that he
was entitled to damages for "past and future medical
expenses, loss of future earnings, and pain and suffering."

A United States District Court in Florida agreed with
the student and awarded him $850,000 in damages. The
defendant appealed the unfavorable decision and
denied any negligent conduct. Instead, the defendant
charged the student with contributory negligence for
failing to use reasonable care for his own safety. The
defendant pointed to a recent ruling of a court in Florida
that ruled that the question of an invitee did not matter
since such a distinction was abolished. In *Camp v. Gulf
Counties Gas Co.*, a Florida court declared:

> This case appears to abolish in Florida the dis-
> tinctions which previously have been drawn re-
> garding the duties owed to invitees, licensees,
> and trespassers, and to substitute therefore a

single duty of reasonable care under the circumstances existing.[7]

The defendant also charged that while the pool was dark, the street light provided sufficient light for the plaintiff to see that the pool was empty. The defendant admitted that it violated the ordinance requiring fencing and locks for gates but strongly denied any "willful and wanton" conduct. The defendant also contended that the district court failed to consider the issue of contributory negligence and requested the higher court to give the question due consideration.

The United States Court of Appeals for the Fifth Circuit reversed the earlier decision and $850,000 award by ordering a new trial. The court stated:

> While the tragedy inherent in the facts presented evokes the sympathy of this Court, the case should have been submitted with instructions based upon these principles of negligence law applicable to the evidence adduced.[8]

One of the judges deplored the new trial because he felt the trial judge "went both too far and not far enough." He commented in his dissent that:

> In this day and time of explosive docket increases it is unfortunate that one of the busiest trial courts in the Fifth Circuit must now re-try the whole case on simple negligence and damages with a prospect of a second appeal to this court whose docket has exponentially increased over 400% since 1960.

---

7. Camp v. Gulf Counties Gas Co., 265 So. 2d 730 (Fla. Dist. Ct. App. 1972).
8. *Supra* note 6.

Before a new trial was held, three weeks after the accident in the pool, the plaintiff died from flu which was complicated by his injury. The case was settled out of court up to the limits of the insurance policy in favor of the plaintiff.

Ponds

The parents of a retarded student in Louisiana sought damages for the tragic drowning death of their son.[9] The boy attended the school for over three years. The school was located on a 50-acre campus with several ponds on it.

The boy worked on the maintenance crew as a part of his training. The school offered vocational experiences in carpentry, masonry, mechanics, etc. Each work group had a supervisor who helped the students but did not always stay with them on a continuous basis. While the supervisor was away from the group, the boy fell into the pond and drowned.

During the trial the question was raised as to whether the school had the duty to provide continuous supervision for the students during the regular day or not. The boy's parents insisted that the school did owe such a duty since the students at the school were retarded.

School officials explained that the school deliberately planned a policy of freedom for the students according to their individual mental and physical abilities. They pointed out that the boy was very familiar with the ponds on campus since he passed them often. They claimed that

9. Hunter v. Evergreen Presbyterian Vocational School, 338 So. 2d 164 (La. App. 1976).

he was not dangerous to himself and did not require special attention. The school authorities indicated that:

> the educational advantages of providing the students some freedom and opportunity to learn self-reliance, and the quality of life advantages of the open space in which students lived and worked, far outweigh the risks of harm attendant, thereto. The risks were minimal and were not unreasonable under the circumstances.

On the other hand, the parents claimed that the unsupervised pond represented an attractive nuisance and contributed to the death of their son. The Court of Appeal of Louisiana responded that:

> Application of the attractive nuisance doctrine is nothing more than nomenclature given to a determination that a defendant has breached its duty of reasonable care for the safety of others by maintaining on its premises an unreasonable and foreseeable hazard to children or others with child-life judgment.

It concluded that the pond existed for years and the boy was aware of it. As such the court felt that the pond did not present a risk or hazard that was either unreasonable or foreseeable to the students. While it found the drowning of the retarded boy deplorable and tragic, the court ruled that the school and its employees were not liable for the boy's unexpected death.

Outings

A fifteen-year-old boy almost drowned in a private Swim Club pool on a school outing. The boy jumped into

the pool and after a few strokes he went under.[10] The
boy's father charged the school district and the Swim
Club with negligent conduct for failing to provide adequate
supervision to the class of twenty-five who were on the
outing. In addition, he accused the Swim Club of failing
to provide lifeguards for supervisory duty.

During the trial, the defendants proved that a lifeguard
was on duty and a second lifeguard was in an area
adjacent to the pool. A physician at the hospital where
the boy was taken indicated that he examined the boy
and found that:

> his pulse was very vigorous and he finally re-
> sponded to admit that he had eaten a large
> dinner before swimming, that he dove off the
> board and that he did not know how to swim.

The Illinois Appellate Court referred to an Illinois
statute which protects the school district from liability
unless the district can be held guilty of "wanton and
willful conduct." It decided that no such conduct existed
in the immediate case. It upheld the lower court's decision
in favor of the defendant school district but reversed the
lower court's verdict for the Swim Club and ordered a
new trial by jury to determine the Swim Club's part of
the accident.

The parents of a six-year-old girl whose leg was crushed
by a log at the beach during a school outing sued the
school district for negligence.[11] The plaintiffs charged
the school district in Oregon with a lack of adequate

---

10. Morrison v. Community Unit School Dist. No. 1, 358 N.E.2d
    389 (Ill. App. 1976).
11. Morris v. Douglas County School Dist., 403 P.2d 775 (Ore.
    1965).

supervision for their young daughter. The circuit court ruled in favor of the injured girl and the school district appealed to the Supreme Court of Oregon.

A teacher and six other adults, including the injured girl's mother took 35 children to the beach on a school day. A log was in a dry area on the sand where the tide had left it. The children were sitting on the log while the teacher was taking their picture. A mother called to the children to get off the log, but no one either heard or paid any attention to the warning. A large wave suddenly hit the beach and the log struck the leg of the girl.

The trial court judge had ruled in favor of the girl by saying:

> The court finds that the child was permitted to play on a log some thirty to fifty feet from the surf, on a beach of substantially level contour, sloping gently upward from the water . . ., on and adjacent to a log which would have a natural tendency to cause the youngsters playing about the log to become distracted from the action of the surf; and, . . . at this self-same time, . . . [the teacher's] supervision was temporarily suspended during a movie-taking operation. . . .

The Supreme Court of Oregon listened to all the testimony and ruled that the teacher failed to furnish the students proper supervision at the time the accident took place. It affirmed the lower court's decision for the injured girl.

Water Skiing

Today it is possible that schools will include water-skiing to the regular physical education curricula or as a part of independent activities such as contracting. It is probable that school authorities will have another high risk area to consider regarding liability. It is expedient to examine two court cases involving waterskiing to determine the attitude of the courts toward injuries that relate to waterskiing.

Annette Harrop was injured in East Canyon Reservoir in Utah when she fell off her skis and was struck by a boat driven by the defendant.[12] The jury was asked to determine whether the defendant failed to keep a proper lookout or whether Annette was guilty of contributory negligence for her failure to keep a lookout of the defendant's boat.

In the state of Utah, assumption of risk is recognized as a defense in cases involving negligence. The Utah Supreme Court ruled in this case, however, that the girl did not assume the risk of the defendant's negligence when he was 80 feet from her and still managed to run into her.

It therefore upheld the lower court's verdict in behalf of the injured girl. It ruled that Annette was not guilty of contributory negligence but the defendant was guilty instead for failing to provide a proper lookout for the girl while she was in the water.

Michael Reddick fell into the water while he was being towed on water skis.[13] He was run over by another boat and died from the injuries he received from the boat's propeller. Both parties charged the other with acts that caused the man's death.

---

12. Harrop v. Beckman, 387 P.2d 554 (Utah 1963).
13. Reddick v. Lindquist, 484 S.W.2d 441 (Tex. App. 1972).

During the trial evidence was produced that revealed that Reddick was trying to improve his technique of waterskiing. The boat towing the plaintiff arrived at the mouth of the lake at the same time the defendant's boat reached it. Reddick was "skiing on a slalom ski" and moving toward the defendant's boat "when he lost his balance and fell into the water." He apparently tried to retrieve his ski and did not see the approaching boat. He turned to his left and was struck by the defendant's boat. The testimony stated that Reddick had no obstruction between himself and the boat to hinder his view of the oncoming boat. He had a lightweight life jacket on at the time but it was not cumbersome and he had the ability to maneuver in the water.

The Court of Civil Appeals of Texas reasoned that the plaintiff had the obligation "to keep a proper lookout for his own safety." It confirmed the lower court's opinion that the deceased was aware of the defendant's boat and that his failure to use reasonable care was the proximate cause of the injury. In so ruling, it favored the defendant.

Summary

Water-related activities such as swimming, waterskiing, fishing, boating and scuba-diving have reached an all-time high as 100 million people participate in some water-related activity each year.

Over 7,000 people drown each year and this represents the second most deaths due to accidents from age 4 to 44 in the United States.

There appears to be very little litigation in water-related accidents, however, although the activities are in the high risk area. In the eight cases considered in this chapter only two verdicts favored the plaintiffs.

It seems that the court's logic is that drowning does not normally occur due to negligence. It reasons that several factors play a major role in accidents or fatalities such as:

1) the inherent dangers of swimming;
2) the possibilities of bodily malfunction on the part of the victim;
3) the lack of control over the swimmers who might contribute to the misadventure; and
4) the victim's own negligence.

8. Independent Activities

Courses in physical education will thus be curtailed or eliminated depending on the degree of 'guess' indulged in by the school authority on what a jury would say about it.[1]

During the 1960's an unprecedented search for innovation in education led to widespread experimentation that produced educational television, team teaching, teacher aides, ungraded schools and programs for the gifted.

A new force has emerged in the seventies that goes beyond the implementation of techniques devised in the sixties. Don Adams and Gerald Reagan in *Schooling and Social Change in America* describe the new approach when they predict that:

> the bureaucratic arrangement of structured schooling must be replaced by guaranteeing more responsibility and freedom for the learner. The deschooled society envisioned presumably allows more meaningful learning to take place and generates new levels of creativity.[2]

Contracting is the innovative practice of permitting a student to sign a contract with a teacher and school to conduct a program of physical activity on an independent basis, usually off campus. It represents a creative attempt

---

1. Bellman v. San Francisco High School Dist., 81 P.2d 894 (Cal. 1938).
2. Don Adams and Gerald Reagan, Schooling and Social Change in Modern America, David McKay Company, Inc., New York, 1972.

in physical education to enable students to plan a course based on their interests, needs and abilities. The participants can set personal goals and then progress at their own pace. Students can use the flexibility of such a program to solve scheduling problems and promote lifetime activities with carry-over value in later life.

Pennsylvania and New York have programs with carefully planned guidelines while California, Maryland, New Jersey, New York, Ohio, Rhode Island and Wisconsin have initiated programs also. Georgia and several other states, report a future interest in contracting when their current curricula are revised. A questionnaire was sent to the 50 state departments of education and several provinces of Canada to determine the status of contracting. (See Appendix B for the copy of the letter and for the replies.)

States that offer contracting include the following activities:

   a. physical fitness or aerobics
   b. archery
   c. bicycling
   d. bowling
   e. golf
   f. fly and bait casting
   g. hiking and camping
   h. orienteering
   i. aquatic activities
   j. dance
   k. handball
   l. skiing
   m. small craft operation
   n. ice skating
   o. roller skating
   p. snow sledding

q. surfing
r. scuba diving
s. tennis
t. weight training

Contracting advocates point out that the flexibility of the informal classes permits the vocational student, the accelerated student and the atypical student the opportunity to participate without the restrictions of formal and structured classes.[3]

An overwhelming number of state departments of education are interested in contracting because it individualizes activities and meets interests and needs of students. These same groups, however, express concern about the legality of such a program and reveal the frustration and insecurity contracting generates.

Contracting With Outside Agencies

Several states rely on outside agencies such as golf courses, riding academies, ballet schools, skiing centers, etc. to teach various activities not available in the particular school.[4] They make it clear that the local board of education should investigate and approve the outside agencies and recommend periodic inspection of the personnel and facilities.

Most school districts require the school board attorney to draw up a contract with the outside agency placing

---

3. *Contracting: An Approach to Providing Flexibility in the Physical Education Program,* Bureau of Curricular Services, Pennsylvania State Dept. of Educ., 1974.
4. *Guidelines for Elementary and Secondary Physical Education Programs,* State Dept. of Educ., 1974.

the responsibility for liability upon the agency and not the school. When the agency receives remuneration for the use of its facilities and instruction it assumes a proprietary function and subsequent responsibility for its conduct. An exception exists when the school district acts as a partner in a joint endeavor with the agency and receives financial support. In this event, the school district is also liable for negligence and liability with the agency.

High Risk Activities

Most school districts use the outside agency to supervise the high risk activities such as aquatics, skiing, skating, snow sledding and tobogganing, surfing, scuba diving, etc. Schools with qualified teachers require supervision and instruction if outside agencies are not used. In a few instances, physical education teachers supervise the activities but the outside agencies do the instructing.

One thing is clear, high risk activities on an independent and unsupervised basis are not recommended. The danger of litigation is high.

Low Risk Activities

There are certain activities that present little danger for the participant. The average student jogs, plays tennis, handball, dances, golfs and hikes with only the normal risk of the activity present. It is reasonable to expect contracting between a teacher and student in these activities without fear of liability.

According to Ruth and Kern Alexander in *Teacher and Torts*,[5] the courts prefer to leave educational and institutional policies to the people who are responsible for school policy rather than judges and juries. In *Bellman v. San Francisco Unified School District* the judge, in a vigorous dissent, said:

> Courses in physical education will thus be curtailed or eliminated depending on the degree of 'guess' indulged in by the school authorities on what a jury would say about it—the directors of the school district cannot be held negligent in prescribing those exercises in view of the common acceptance of the course by others.[6]

Guidelines for Contracting

Guidelines vary with the various states as individual differences exist in philosophy and organization. Pennsylvania has one of the most complete sets of guidelines that are worthy of consideration. The guidelines include the following suggestions:

1. The contract method should receive approval from the local school board. Such a contract should be in written form and agreed upon by the student, the physical education teacher and the administration.
2. Contracts should be written for activities that are part of the planned course of study.
3. Contracts should state objectives and description of the desired activity. It should

---

5. Ruth and Kern Alexander, Teachers and Torts, Maxwell Publishing Co., Middletown, Kentucky.
6. *Supra* note 1.

include the location, available resources, personnel and expected outcomes for the student. Evaluative criteria should be clearly stated, including an assessment of contract effectiveness.

4. Contracts should be developed, monitored and verified by a certified physical education instructor. Noncertified personnel may be utilized when sanctioned by statute.

5. Contracts should be in writing, signed by the student, school district representative and the parent or guardian.

6. Contracts should consider duration of contract, dates and locations for evaluation of student progress, estimated cost to student (if any) insurance and liability coverage which identified insured and insuror, travel considerations, and equipment and materials required.[7] (For the complete manual see Appendix B.)

Statutory Sanction

One of the safeguards a state department can include in contracting is the legislative inclusion in the statutes or school code of the program. It can define contracting and the use of noncertified instructors.

California's legislature amended its education code to include contract programs. The amended code gives validity to the contract program by mandating that:

> For the purpose of computing the average daily attendance of high school students in a school district, attendance shall include pupil

---

7. *Contracting: An Approach to Providing Flexibility in the Physical Education Program, supra* note 3.

activities, carried on independently, should reduce the school's responsibility and standard of care since the activities are those normally attributed to everyday activities and offer little if any foreseeable risk.

Several states, among them California, Maryland, New Jersey, New York, Ohio, Rhode Island, Wisconsin, have taken leadership in developing guidelines for contracting. Other states indicate interest in future programs.

The question of legal liability is a pressing one and one that the various states admit confuses them. Statutory sanction and liability insurance are the most reliable safeguards while parental waivers offer little, if any, protection. Future decisions by the courts should be watched for guidance.

Summation

Physical education activities have been the leading source of school-related accidents for years. As a result, litigation in physical education has been high. Today the rise in court cases related to physical education results, not only from pupil injuries, but for a variety of reasons. The courts are asked to adjudicate disputes that range from a teacher's refusal to supervise an extracurricular activity to the teacher's refusal to conform to a required dress code.

Another recent change is the tremendous increase in the size of personal injury awards as million dollar awards are becoming commonplace.

The courts do not use a mathematical formula to determine the size of the awards but use various criteria such as the person's age, talents, life expectancy and ability to earn a living before and after the injury. The court's intention is to restore the finances and health of an injured person to the status that existed before the accident.

The trend today is for the plaintiff to name as many people as possible in a lawsuit in the hope that someone will be found negligent and subject to damages.

The present-day court is more sympathetic to teachers while the public is less tolerant and demands a higher standard of care than ever before. In fact, what was once considered reasonable may now be negligence.

Some authorities in school law insist that teachers are sued more than any other group while others argue that they are "judgment-proof" because they often lack the money to pay huge awards. At any rate, both groups agree that no defendant has been found guilty by the courts when there was evidence that the defendant acted with caution in the performance of his duty.

In injury cases, absence of the teacher is the leading charge. Recently, the court has made it clear that absence alone does not constitute negligence. It has ruled that it would be unreasonable for a teacher to call for outside assistance every time he or she wanted to leave for a short time. The court does expect a teacher to use sound judgment before a class is left unsupervised. It considers the age and type of student in the class, the time, place, equipment, length of the absence and the reason for the absence before it decides on a case.

The court realizes that physical education encompasses risks and hazards by its very nature and therefore it cannot be made "child-proof."

It does require a teacher in high risk activities, such as gymnastics, to properly instruct, prepare and warn students of the activity. It expects teachers to use judgment in assigning students' activities by ability. The court expects teachers to foresee danger and act to protect students from it.

In other issues than pupil injury, the court gives the local school board tremendous latitude in formulating policy. A teacher is expected to conform to rules regarding dress and appearance. The court cautions the school board that the teacher's dress or appearance must be detrimental to the educational process before the board acts.

The court prohibits sex bias in hiring procedures, tenure, career ladders and working conditions. It consistently rules that the local officials are more qualified to decide what is best for a school system than any court. It therefore puts policy making decisions on local officials.

A school board is responsible for adopting safe rules of conduct and enforcing them. When a defect exists on the premises or with equipment, there must be time for the school to know the condition existed and repair it before liability can be established.

School districts in most states still enjoy immunity although many exceptions such as liability insurance, safe-place statutes and public building exceptions have modified the doctrine. The majority of court cases are litigated in states that have abrogated the immunity doctrine and in many instances these districts are expected to be the insurer of the safety of the students.

The administrator is one step removed from the student and therefore is not as vulnerable to a lawsuit as the teacher. The administrator is responsible for the safe operation of the school. The administrator is not liable, however, for non-school activities conducted off-campus.

Water-related activities are responsible for the second highest death rate by accidents for persons 4 to 44 years of age. There is a surprising lack of litigation although the activities are high risk. The court reasons that drowning and other accidents are usually not caused by negligence and therefore liability is not a factor.

New physical education programs such as contracting are popular and spreading rapidly in many states. Guidelines are available but court decisions are lacking to provide the position of the court in such programs. The area will bear watching for future litigation.

If present trends continue liability cases in physical education will increase and awards will continue to rise to unprecedented levels.

The American law of negligence is not to be found in a written code of laws but is based upon precedent or established modes of legal procedure. A previous judicial decision is used as a basis for subsequent decisions and negligence is viewed against this background. There are no sure criteria for determining what is negligent action and what is not since each case stands individually on its own merit. *The key to liability is the presence of negligence.*

Appendix A

State by State Synopsis of Immunity

1.	Alabama	Sovereign immunity, total	256 So. 2d 281 (1972)
		Governmental immunity, unknown	
		Charitable immunity, total	184 So. 2d 825 (1966)
2.	Alaska	Sov. imm., statutory waiver	A.S. § 09. 50.250
		Gov. imm., '' ''	''
		Char. imm., unknown	
3.	Arkansas	Sov. imm., total	407 S.W.2d 917 (1966)
		Gov. imm., unknown	
		Char. imm., total	492 S.W.2d 243 (1969)
4.	Arizona	Sov. imm., gov't prop.	381 P.2d 107 (1963)
		Gov. imm., '' ''	'' '' '' ''
		Char. imm., none	243 P.2d 455 (1952)
5.	California	Sov. imm., Tort Claims Act	
		Gov. imm., '' '' Act	
		Char. imm., none	232 P.2d 241 (1951)
6.	Colorado	Sov. imm., gov't prop.	482 P.2d 966 (1972)
		Gov. imm., '' ''	'' '' '' ''
		Char. imm., none	355 P.2d 1078 (1961)
7.	Connecticut	Sov. imm., total	122 A.2d 30 (1956)
		Gov. imm., unknown	
		Char. imm., total	229 A.2d 32 (1967)
8.	Delaware	Sov. imm., total	197 A.2d 734 (1964)
		Gov. imm., unknown	
		Char. imm., unknown	
9.	District of Columbia	Sov. imm., unknown	
		Gov. imm., judicial abrogation	
		Char. imm., none	251 F. Supp. 614 (D.D.C. 1966)
10.	Florida	Sov. imm., total	290 So. 2d 532 (1974)
		Gov. imm., unknown	
		Char. imm., unknown	
11.	Georgia	Sov. imm., total insurance waiver	149 S.E.2d 530 (1966)
		Gov. imm., gov't prop., ins. waiver	147 S.E.2d 789 (1966)
		Char. imm., limited to char. assets	188 S.E.2d 915 (1972)

12. Hawaii	Sov. imm., statutory waiver	H.R.S. §§ 662-1 et seq.
	Gov. imm., '' ''	
	Char. imm., unknown	
13. Idaho	Sov. imm., gov't prop.	473 P.2d 937 (1970)
	Gov. imm., '' ''	487 P.2d 936 (1971)
	Char. imm., none	421 P.2d 745 (1967)
14. Illinois	Sov. imm., total	Const. art. 4, § 26
	Gov. imm., gov't prop.	163 N.E.2d 89 (1959)
	Char., imm., none	257 N.E.2d 239 (1970)
15. Indiana	Sov. imm., gov't prop.	284 N.E.2d 733 (1972)
	Gov. imm., '' ''	112 N.E.2d 891 (1953)
	Char. imm., none	237 N.E.2d 242 (1968)
16. Iowa	Sov. imm., Tort Claims Act, min.-dis.	I.C.A. §§ 25A.1 et seq.
	Gov. imm., Tort Claims Act, min.-dis.	
	Char. imm., none	266 F. Supp. 129 (D.C. Iowa 1964)
17. Kansas	Sov. imm., judicial abrogation, legislation this year	
	Gov. imm., gov't prop.	
	Char. imm., none	
18. Kentucky	Sov. imm., total—may be legislative waiver in some cases	418 S.W.2d 407 (1967)
	Gov. imm., total—may be legislative waiver in some cases	
	Char. imm., limited	348 S.W.2d 930 (1961)
19. Louisiana	Sov. imm., total	263 So. 2d 113 (1972)
	Gov. imm., gov't prop.	214 So. 2d 153 (1968)
	Char. imm., none	289 So. 2d 88 (1974)
20. Maine	Sov. imm., total-court advised leg. to take action in changing the law	286 A.2d 344 (1972)
	Gov. imm., total-court advised leg. to take action in changing the law	'' '' '' ''
	Char. imm., total, ins. waiver	297 A.2d 98 (1972)

21. Maryland	Sov. imm., statutory enactment	
	Gov. imm., '' ''	
	Char. imm., total	398 F.2d 226
		(D.C. Md. 1972)
22. Massachusetts	Sov. imm., total?-possibly some	198 N.E.2d 420 (1964)
	leg. enactment	
	Gov. imm., total?-possibly some	
	leg. enactment	
	Char. imm., statutory abolition	M.G.L.A. c. 231, § 85
23. Michigan	Sov. imm., Tort Claims Act	M.C.L.A. § 691.1401
	Gov. imm., gov't prop.	213 N.W.2d 784 (1973)
	Char. imm., none	165 N.W.2d 326 (1968)
24. Minnesota	Sov. imm., total	322 F. Supp. 33 (1971)
	Gov. imm., min.-dis.	118 N.W.2d 795 (1962)
	Char. imm., none	115 N.W.2d 666 (1961)
25. Mississippi	Sov. imm., total, ins. waiver	220 So. 2d 349 (1969)
	Gov. imm., gov't prop., ins.	264 So. 2d 892 (1972)
	waiver	
	Char. imm., unknown	
26. Missouri	Sov. imm., total, ins. waiver	521 S.W.2d 403 (1975)
	Gov. imm., '' '' ''	
	Char. imm., statutory abolition	R.S. Mo. § 537.100
27. Montana	Sov. imm., gov't prop.	Const. art. 2, § 8
	Gov. imm., '' ''	480 P.2d 826 (1971)
	Char. imm., none	193 F. Supp. (D.C. Mont.
		1961)
28. Nebraska	Sov. imm., unknown	
	Gov. imm., gov't prop.	169 N.W.2d 286 (1969)
	Char. imm., none	141 N.W.2d 852 (1966)
29. Nevada	Sov. imm., Tort Claims Act,	N.R.S. §§ 41.031 et seq.
	min.-dis.	
	Gov. imm., Tort Claims Act,	
	min.-dis.	
	Char. imm., unknown	
30. New Hampshire	Sov. imm., total, ins. waiver	341 A.2d 282 (1975)
(leg. is now consider-	Gov. imm., unknown, '' ''	
ing enactment)	Char. imm., none	193 A.2d 788 (1963)

31. New Jersey	Sov. imm., Tort Claims Act Gov. imm., '' '' '' Char. imm., statutory enactment	N.J.S.A. §§ 59:1-3 N.J.S.A. §§ 2A:53A et

32. New Mexico	Sov. imm., recently abolished,
	    ins. waiver
	Gov. imm., recently abolished,
	    ins. waiver
	Char. imm., none	

33. New York	Sov. imm., Tort Claims Act,
	    gov't prop.
	Gov. imm., Tort Claims Act,
	    gov't prop.
	Char. imm., none
		
		Const. art. 1, § 16

34. North Carolina	Sov. imm., Tort Claims Act Gov. imm., '' '' '' Char. imm., not as to em- ployees	N.C.G.S. §§ 143-291 et 169 S.E.2d 253 (1969)
35. North Dakota	Sov. imm., total, ins. waiver Gov. imm., unknown Char. imm., unknown	115 N.W.2d 334 (1962)
36. Ohio	Sov. imm., total, ins. waiver- court told leg. to take action Gov. imm., unknown-court told leg. to take action Char. imm., limited	298 N.W.2d 542 (1973) 399 N.E.2d 924 (1975)
37. Oklahoma	Sov. imm., total Gov. imm., statutory waiver Char. imm., unknown	514 P.2d 938 (1973)

38. Oregon	Sov. imm., Tort Claims Act,
	    min.-dis.
	Gov. imm., Tort Claims Act,
	    min.-dis.
	Char. imm., none
		O.R.S. §§ 30.260-30.330
		
		385 P.2d 617 (1963)

39. Pennsylvania	Sov. imm., Tort Claims Act,
	    gov't prop.
	Gov. imm., Tort Claims Act,
	    gov't prop.
	Char. imm., none
		71 P.S. § 562
		
		267 A.2d 867 (1970)

40. Rhode Island	Sov. imm., statutory waiver	Gen. Laws 1956, §§ 9-31-1 et seq.
	Gov. imm., '' ''	
	Char. imm., none	265 A.2d 733 (1970)
41. South Carolina	Sov. imm., total	
	Gov. imm., total	204 S.E.2d 384 (1974)
	Char. imm., total	211 S.E.2d 241 (1975)
42. South Dakota	Sov. imm., total	
	Gov. imm., total	
	Char. imm., unknown	145 N.W.2d 524 (1966)
43. Tennessee	Sov. imm., total	399 S.W.2d 776 (1965)
	Gov. imm., gov't prop.	225 S.W.2d 49 (1949)
	Char. imm., total	196 F. Supp. 114 (D.C. Tenn. 1961)
44. Texas	Sov. imm., Tort Claims Act, but schools still immune	T.R.C.S.A. art. 6252-19
	Gov. imm., Torts Claims Act, but schools still immune	
	Char. imm., none	470 S.W.2d 311 (1968)
45. Utah	Sov. imm., statutory waiver, gov't prop.	U.C.A. 1953, § 63-30-10
	Gov. imm., statutory waiver, gov't prop.	
	Char. imm., none	118 F.2d 836 (10th Cir. 1941)
46. Vermont	Sov. imm., total, ins. waiver	
	Gov. imm., '' '' ''	
	Char. imm., unknown	
47. Virginia	Sov. imm., total?-some question as to a min.-dis. distinction	200 S.E.2d 569 (1973)
	Gov. imm., total? - some question as to a min.-dis. distinction	
	Char. imm., limited	395 F.2d 381 (1968)
48. Washington	Sov. imm., Tort Claims Act, min.-dis.	R.C.W.A. §§ 4.92-090
	Gov. imm., Tort Claims Act, min.-dis.	
	Char. imm., none	396 P.2d 546 (1964)

49. West Virginia	Sov. imm., total, ins. waiver	
	Gov. imm., ″ , ″ ″	
	Char. imm., none	143 S.E.2d 154 (1965)
50. Wisconsin	Sov. imm., Tort Claims Act	184 N.W.2d 99 (1971)
	for autos & aircraft only	
	Gov. imm., unknown	W.S.A. § 114.065
	Char. imm., none	183 N.W.2d 81 (1971)
51. Wyoming	Sov. imm., total, ins. waiver	
	Gov. imm., gov't prop.	389 P.2d 23 (1964)
	Char. imm., limited	469 P.2d 409 (1970)

See also JAMES PALMER, THE CASE OF THE DISAPPEARING IMMUNITIES, March, 1976.

Appendix B

Questionnaire and Survey by States on Contracting

Department of Athletics
December 22, 1975

Fred V. Hein
Director, Department of Health Education
American Medical Association
755 Wingate Road
Glen Ellyn, Illinois   60137

Dear Dr. Hein:

I am preparing a paper on the liability involved in a program of independent activity or the contract method of physical education.

Many administrators and teachers have expressed a deep concern regarding the responsibility in such a program.

I would be most grateful if you would send me any material you have on such a program in your state. Do you have any method devised for the protection of the teachers involved in an independent program of physical education?

With kindest regards, I am

Sincerely yours,

Herb Appenzeller
Athletic Director
Professor of Education

HA/sjk

Guilford College • Post Office Box 8066
Greensboro, North Carolina 27410

Response to Letter Regarding Contracting:

Arizona

each district is autonomous and makes its own policies and handles programs and problems differently.

California

two programs relative to contracting:
(a) students report off-campus but under the supervision of a certified teacher even though the teacher may not teach the class
(b) independent study off campus where the student only reports the progress made to the teacher. Written reports for evaluation of the total work accomplished is required.

California relies on insurance although several carriers cancelled the policy regarding contracting and independent study. It also depends on parental liability release forms but questions their validity. California defines by statute the independent study program.

Delaware

material not available at the state level. There is deep concern regarding the responsibility for such a program. Each school district has the responsibility for liability insurance.

District of Columbia

no formal program in the District of Columbia for contracting although a few teachers have experimented with it with good results.

Florida

lack of material on subject. Each teacher is responsible for the safety of the students during any assigned activity.

Maryland

physical education is required each year student is in school. This requirement may be achieved by an individualized approved program involving contracting. In approved noncredit in-school or out-of-school participation, the minimum aggregate hours for the year should be computed on the basis of two periods per week. Noncredit activities may include participation in an individual interest activity or activities, such as swimming, jogging, cycling, dancing, weight training and gymnastics, varsity sports programs, intramural activities or other planned, diversified and personalized activities.

Michigan
no program reported

Minnesota
state-wide material not available but if they required such activities such as rock climbing, there would be only accepted standards or prerequisites to enter the course.

Missouri
students must be taught or supervised by certified teachers during the regular school day. No contracting to date. They do not visualize any problems if the program is well designed and careful planning is undertaken. Setting up contracting for all students is ridiculous. Such a program must be in writing.

New Jersey
advise school district to consult their attorneys who can determine acceptable outside agencies. Contracts with outside agencies must be signed with a liability clause stipulated. In addition, parental permission slips are required.

New York
useful alternatives but contracting must be considered in light of possible litigation and insurance coverage.

> For students in grades 10 through 12 only, allowing a time comparable to 2½ hours per week in an activity conducted outside of the school domain can be accepted as meeting the physical education requirements so long as the agency or organization and the personnel doing the instructing have been investigated and approved by the board of education. Such approvals should be periodically reviewed. This type of approval should only be given for those activities that are not ordinarily provided or cannot be provided by the school. Where approval for such programs are given, there should be a specified period of time

indicated, such as a marking period or semester. Such approvals should also be reviewed periodically. Agencies or organizations approved could include: golf courses, riding academies, ballet schools, skiing centers, etc. In the event that a school is considering such an option, it is recommended that the school consult its counsel and insurance carrier for guidance. (N.Y. State Dept. Guidelines for Phys. Educ. Program)

North Carolina

no specific material on subject

Ohio

the state has developed several programs such as:
(a) lifetime sports
(b) leisure education
(c) outdoor adventure activities
The responsibility is on the local school district. Insurance is individual teacher's responsibility.

Oklahoma

has not devised a particular method. Strongly recommend parental permission slips explaining the activity and limits of supervision. Recommend that teachers carry liability insurance. Not suit conscious but want insurance so that activities are not limited due to fear of lawsuit.

Ontario

do not have contracting but would advise teachers in such programs to be covered with adequate insurance.

Oregon

no specific regulations covering contracting but use some legal requirements as they pertain to other instructional programs.

Pennsylvania

has a well-defined and carefully organized plan for contracting. The program is treated like the band, forensics and other traveling activities.

Rhode Island

no additional coverage for such programs. Teachers are generally covered by school district from $100,000 to $300,000. In addition there is an excess general liability coverage up to one million dollars.

Texas

such a program would be on an elective basis if adopted. Parental permission would be required.

Utah

no material on the subject. Traditional guidelines require the presence of a teacher as an instructor or in an advisory role. There are students who work independently, jogging, weight training and in lifetime sports.

Vermont

utilizes professional instructors in skiing in various parts of the state to train students in grades 1-12 in skiing. An example is the Stowe Ski Program in which students are taught free and classed by ability. Volunteers from the community assist the instructors. It offers snowskiing, bowling, swimming and snowmobiling also.

Virginia

(a) contract to outside agency such activities as horsemanship, riflery, boating, etc.

(b) contract between teacher and student in the gathering of research and not a risk activity such as a physical activity.

Washington

put emphasis on teacher training institutions to prepare future teachers for teaching and coaching. Encourages in-service training in legal liability.

Wisconsin

offers contracting to "better" students. Tends to parallel honor study halls and use of community resources for teaching academic classes. The state officials believe that the orientation of students in the safety measures appropriate to the activity involved, plus reasonable concern and preparation for supervision of students should satisfy the foreseeability factor in this type of teaching.

Wyoming

when a teacher signs up with the Wyoming Education Association they are covered whether the course is a regular one or contracting.

SOQUEL HIGH SCHOOL
Santa Cruz High School District
401 Old San Jose Road
Soquel, California   95073

SOQUEL HIGH — PHYSICAL EDUCATION DEPARTMENT
ACTIVITY CONTRACT

SCHOOL YEAR 19. . — 19. .   . . . . REPORT PERIOD

I . . . . am contracting with . . . .
        (name)   (establishment)

for 30 hours of instruction in . . . . I understand
                                    (activity)

that in the event I fail to meet the requirements of the instructor of
the activity, I will not only fail to receive credit, but will forfeit any
fees paid to the establishment involved.

                    . . . .
                    student signature

. . . .
P.E. Period   Year

. . . .
Parent Approval   Instructor Approval

CONTRACT PHYSICAL EDUCATION ACTIVITIES

SCUBA   1st report period 1974

CONTRACTING AGENCY—O'Neill's Dive Shop

INSTRUCTOR—John Hauck, O'Neills

PLACE—Soquel High Pool and Classroom 112

HOURS—7:00—9:00 p.m.

MEETING DATES   September—16, 17, 18, 23, 24, 25, 30
                  October—1, 2, 7, 8, 9, 14, 15, 16, 21, 22, 23
                  2 hour class sessions

FEES—There is no fee for the class, however, each student must supply his own mask, snorkel and fins. (Approximate cost $25.00) Although not a part of the class, there will be opportunity for those interested to obtain an ocean checkout. A diving card will be awarded to those who successfully complete this checkout. Air and other SCUBA equipment may not be purchased without a diving card. There is a fee of $25.00 for the ocean checkout.

Class Limit—20 students

CONTRACT PHYSICAL EDUCATION ACTIVITIES

BOWLING

CONTRACTING AGENCY—Surf Bowl

INSTRUCTOR—Dusty Harmon, Surf Bowl

PLACE—Surf Bowl, 115 Cliff St., Santa Cruz

HOURS—3:30—5:30 p.m.

MEETING DATES   September—16, 19, 20, 23, 24, 26, 27, 30
October—3, 4, 7, 8, 10, 11, 14, 15, 17, 18
2 hour class sessions

FEE—$11.70 payable to Surf Bowl

Transportation to and from Surf Bowl will be provided by student
Class Limit—40 students

TABLE OF CASES

Christofides v. Hellenic Eastern Orthodox Christian Church of New York, 227 N.Y.S.2d 946 (N.Y. Mun. Ct. 1962), ch. 2, n. 11.

Cioffi v. Board of Educ. of City of New York, 278 N.Y.S.2d 249 (N.Y. App. Div. 1967), ch. 3, n. 24.

Cirillo v. City of Milwaukee, 150 N.W.2d 460 (Wis. 1967), ch. 3, n. 3.

Clinchfield R.R. Co. v. Forbes, 417 S.W.2d 210 (Tenn. 1967), ch. 1, nn. 18, 19.

Coates v. Tacoma School Dist. No. 10, 347 P.2d 1093 (Wash. 1960), ch. 2, n. 13.

Cody v. Southfield-Lathrup School Dist., 181 N.W.2d 81 (Mich App. 1970), ch. 6, n. 7.

Conway v. Saint Gregory's Parochial School, 235 N.E.2d 217 (N.Y. 1968), ch. 3, n. 22.

Crossen v. Board of Educ. of City of New York, 359 N.Y.S.2d 316 (N.Y. App. Div. 1974), ch. 3, n. 23.

Cumberland College v. Gaines, 432 S.W.2d 650 (Ky. 1968), ch. 6, n. 23.

Daniel v. West Jersey S.R.R., 84 N.J.L. 685 (N.J. 1937), ch. 3, n. 9.

Darrow v. West Genessee Central School Dist., 342 N.Y.S.2d 611 (N.Y. App. Div. 1973), ch. 3, n. 33.

District of Columbia v. Washington, 332 A.2d 347 (D.C. 1975), ch. 6, n. 9.

Durham v. Commonwealth of Kentucky, 406 S.W.2d 858 (Ky. 1966), ch. 7, n. 4.

East Hartford Educ. Ass'n v. Board of Educ. of Town of East Hartford, 405 F. Supp. 94 (D. Conn. 1975), ch. 4, nn. 10, 14, 15.

Faber v. Roelofs, 212 N.W.2d 856 (Minn. 1973), ch. 6, n. 20.

Flournoy v. McComas, 488 P.2d 1104 (Colo. 1971), ch. 2, n. 18.

Fosselman v. Waterloo Community School Dist. in County of Black Hawk, 229 N.W.2d 280 (Iowa 1975), ch. 3, n. 25.

Goldstein v. Board of Educ. of Union Free School Dist. No. 23, Town of Hempstead, 278 N.Y.S.2d 224 (N.Y. 1966), ch. 6, nn. 12, 14.

Guerrieri v. Tyson, 24 A.2d 468 (Pa. 1942), ch. 1, n. 9.

Harrington v. Vandalia-Butler Bd. of Educ., 418 F. Supp. 603 (S.D. Ohio 1976), ch. 4, n. 7.

Harrop v. Beckman, 387 P.2d 554 (Utah 1963), ch. 7, n. 12.

Zaepfel v. City of Yonkers, 392 N.Y.S.2d 336 (N.Y. App. Div. 1977), ch. 6, n. 2.

Zarba v. Lane, 76 N.E.2d 318 (Mass. 1947), ch. 8, n. 13.

Zawadski v. Taylor, 246 N.W.2d 161 (Mich. App. 1976), ch. 6, n. 8.

Index

A

E

F

W

WAIVERS.
  Parental permission slips, pp. 148 to 150.
WATER-RELATED ACCIDENTS.
  Causes generally, p. 140.
  Off-campus activities, pp. 135 to 137.
  Ponds, pp. 134, 135.
  Swimming pools, pp. 128 to 134.
  Water skiing, pp. 137 to 139.
WATER SKIING.
  Accidents, pp. 137 to 139.
WRESTLING, pp. 2, 60.